RED NIGHT

On that ripening moon,
flames and smoke

ate the sky, swallowing
its one white eye.

The coyotes' bacchanal
tearing up the night, was

silenced by the
reddened light.

And the floating ones
just earlier that day,

did those red-tailed hawks
bank their wings and

simply glide away?
Where is he now perched,

that midnight owl with
his laconic note—

Carrier of night
inside his throat.

— *Kiera Van Gelder*

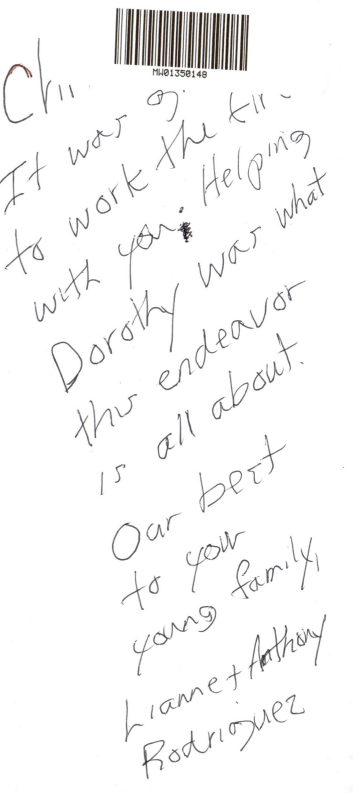

FROM THE FIRE

Ojai Reflects on the Thomas Fire

Elizabeth Rose and Deva Temple

FROM THE FIRE
Ojai Reflects on the Thomas Fire

Elizabeth Rose and Deva Temple

Published by Elizabeth Rose and Deva Temple
www.fromthefirebook.com

Printed by V3 Printing, Oxnard, California

ISBN 978-0-692-17669-3 (softcover)
ISBN 978-0-692-17700-6 (hardcover)
Library of Congress Control Number 2018909901

Front cover: photograph by Mark Anthony
Back cover: photograph by Nathan Wickstrum

Front cover design by Deva Temple
Book design by Deva Temple and Elizabeth Rose

Copyright © 2018, Elizabeth Rose and Deva Temple. All rights reserved. No part of this publication may be reproduced, distributed or transmitted in any form or by any means, electronic or mechanical, including photocopying, recording or by any information storage and retrieval system, without written permission from the publisher. All creators of original content in this publication—photographs, poetry, prose, reflection, artwork images—retain their original copyright and have given us a limited use license for the purpose of this publication.

Although we have made every effort to ensure that the information in this book was correct at press time, including the correct names of all photographers, artists, writers and those we spoke with directly for this book, we do not assume and hereby disclaim any liability to any party for any loss, damage or disruption caused by errors or omissions, whether such errors or omissions result from negligence, accident or any other cause.

TABLE OF CONTENTS

page 11 .... The Thomas Fire

page 33 .... From The Flames

page 83 .... Into The Ashes

page 125 .... Our Community Comes Together

page 179 .... Celebrating Regrowth

Front cover: photograph by Mark Anthony
Back cover: photograph by Nathan Wickstrum
Page ii: photograph by Jeff D. Muth
Page vi: photograph by Stacy Ruppel

THANKS AND GRATITUDE

We would not have been able to create this beautiful book without the support of so many generous and loving people.

We are so thankful to all those who submitted to FROM THE FIRE. We are deeply grateful and humbled that our community shared with open heart and we are truly appreciative of every submission we received. We received over 900 submissions of images and artwork, over 40 writings and we engaged in 45 interviews with members of the Ojai community. This enormous body of photographs, writings, art and reflection means that we could not include every submission in the final book. It was incredibly difficult to decide what became a part of FROM THE FIRE when we have been entrusted with the truth of so many people's experiences. We have created a website—www.fromthefirebook.com—and every person who submitted to FROM THE FIRE will have a page on this site. Moreover, it is our intention that any future submissions will also find a home here. The Thomas Fire forever changed our landscape and ourselves. Let us continue to honor this transformation by carrying on our story. We invite our entire community to connect with us as we move forward. Share with us your thoughts and reflections, your photographs and artwork, so that we may continue to engage in that sweet connection that rose out of the flames of the Thomas Fire.

Special thanks to the following people for your generous giving of time and support, for your constant enthusiasm and for your ever-present belief in this beautiful book. We could not have done this without you.

We are eternally grateful to our editors—Soni Wright, Karal Gregory, Julia Thomsen, Kiera Van Gelder, Teagan Rose, Jennifer Karofsky, Adam Karofsky—for working through the writings and interviews, poems and prose, before we even started putting anything into book form. And then, when all was done and our creation was a book, we passed it to Doug Adrianson, Julia Thomsen, Garth Rose, Teagan Rose and Amy Schneider who painstakingly read through the entire book, catching typos, extra spaces, incorrect formatting, and so much more, and then gently shared the damage with us. And to our last look editors who eyeballed spacing and formatting and caught those last, stubborn typos that hid from all of us—Julia Thomsen, Deborah Tutnauer, Teagan Rose and Terence Carfrae. We understand how much there was to read and are so appreciative of all of you for your time and commitment to this project.

Thank you to Amy Schneider and David Reeser of Ojai Digital. So much appreciation to Amy for not only your editing prowess but also your constant support and guidance during the many months we worked on this book. For your willingness to answer all of our questions through to the end, we are eternally grateful. And to David for your help with ISBN numbers and our many photograph resolution challenges, and your patient support each time we showed up in your office.

Thank you so much, Rick Monzon, for your enthusiasm for this book, the design of our flyers and for your photoshop expertise on those few photos that needed that extra support.

Thank you, Deborah Lyon, for your beautiful photographs of many of the artists' work included in this book.

Thank you to Norman Clayton of Classic Letterpress, for your enthusiasm for this project at its very early stages and for introducing us to Tom Hinkle at V3 Printing.

We could not have created this book without the support, guidance and generous pricing from V3 Printing in Oxnard, California. Tom Hinkle, we are so grateful. Your quick response to our many emails, your willingness to meet in person to go over formatting and your patience throughout this process is so very appreciated. Steve Alkazian, thank you for your guidance on how best to prepare our book for printing, for working through the book, checking photo quality and printing resolution and for the many times we needed help with InDesign. And to Kristy Gomez—whether over email or in person, we are so thankful for your constant communication and support of this project. This book needed to be as beautiful as the subject is important. V3 Printing produced such a book for us.

Our deepest thanks to Vaughn Montgomery and Laurie Cornell of Greater Goods for your willingness to partner with us on this project. We wanted to be able to give back to our community, to those still struggling from the lasting effects of the Thomas Fire and to all those in need as we move forward. Working with Greater Goods allows us to do just that. Thank you for your willingness to integrate this project into your current structure. We are so honored to be able to support the Greater Goods Relief Fund.

Thank you to Chris Cohen for your legal guidance as we navigated how to best work with Greater Goods. We appreciate you offering your time to support this project.

Thank you, Rebecca Adams, for your patience in explaining the many income and sales tax nuances of selling a book.

And finally, to our beautiful husbands, Garth Rose and Sean Goddard. We are so blessed by your constant love and support during the many months that we were deeply absorbed in the creation of this book. We could not have done this without each of you.

THE INTERVIEWS

The interviews are a collection of conversations with members of the Ojai community—individuals, organizations and businesses—sharing their own, unique experiences through the Thomas Fire. Each interview includes the date we spoke with each person—whether two months or seven months after the fire the images remain clear, the details still fresh in the mind, the emotions raw.

The same questions were asked: what was happening when the fire started, where did you go and what did you do, and how did you feel? The conversations were recorded and then transcribed with the intention of keeping the lilt of the voice, the rhythm of the sentence, the essence of each person as they shared their experience with us. The goal was to capture who each person is along with honoring their story and offering the reader many different perspectives of the Thomas Fire. By experiencing the fire through so many eyes, perhaps we can know this fire more fully.

For a map of the locations referenced in this book please visit www.fromthefirebook.com

INTRODUCTION

FROM THE FIRE is a collection of photographs, writings, art and reflection that represent the personal experiences of the Ojai community through the Thomas Fire. From the flames into the ashes to the renewal of our land and our community, this book documents the devastation and loss created by this fire while capturing the hope and possibility and the coming together of the Ojai community.

The idea for this book came as we watched our town ravaged by flames, as we saw the fire burning, as we breathed the smoke, as we feared for ourselves and for the fates of those we love, as we watched the land turn from green to red to black and gray, as we saw what was left in the aftermath... trees were stripped naked, land denuded, barren, empty. And in the most surprising places we found artifacts, indications of lives lived in places lost to the flames. We witnessed the powerful coming together of our community, in person and online as message boards and websites sprang up and people networked, sharing information in real time. We witnessed the outpouring of support, love, grief and generosity that flooded our community. We were touched with the story our community told as the fire was burning and, in the aftermath, with the story of generosity and connection that continues still, a story that challenges the narrative that we are inherently selfish.

The depth of feeling that we have experienced culling through the many submissions that we received for this book is profound. This was not an easy book to create. Working on it brought us face to face with the grief of those who lost homes and animals in the fire and kept us in touch with our own trauma. It would have been easier to move on, to try to put it behind us, but we wanted to create something that would tell a story bigger than our own grief. The rewards we have received have been innumerable. We have made new friends. We have comforted and been comforted. We have borne witness to the myriad of threads and images that weave together the tapestry of this land and of the Ojai community. Our hearts have become sanctuaries for tragedy, inspiration, loss, love and rebirth.

The fire was an invitation to stop and to remember what it is that we love most even as it was an invitation to grieve what was lost. Our hearts beat in the emotional expansion of love and the contraction of grief, ever opening and closing. We became stronger, more capable, when we allowed the fullness of our love and our grief to show up. So often grief is a private emotion, but together as a community we have held each other through it all. That willingness to co-feel with one another has brought us gifts we are still discovering.

The Thomas Fire is now a part of our history and the opportunity to share the experiences that we had, individually and together as a community, is important. Because the Thomas Fire was more than just a fire. It was a hallowed burning of our sacred land that stripped away layers from the Earth and within each of us. This fire was a catalyst for transformation and change, for insight into the suffering that all people encounter in this life. It was an opportunity to become bigger than we were before, and to embody more of our potential as individuals and as community members.

The two of us entered into this project both knowing how special our town is. While we came to this feeling from two very different places, Deva having grown up here and Elizabeth moving here in the summer of 2013, we have been uplifted by the deep love and support that has been shared during and after the Thomas Fire, a giving of self that continues still. We are left with the ever-present belief in the resilient beauty and the powerful community that is Ojai. We are honored to be the stewards of our collective stories, with you, and with the land, plants and animals of this valley and region.

☙ *Elizabeth Rose and Deva Temple*

DEDICATED TO THE COMMUNITY OF OJAI
TO THOSE WHO FOUGHT THE THOMAS FIRE
AND
TO ALL COMMUNITIES THAT FACE SUCH DISASTER

May the ashes make a gorgeous bed for new dreams to take root for humanity.

≽ Emily Burger

Opposite page: photograph by Esther van der Werf

The Thomas Fire

THE BEAST

In the darkness of the night, the Beast was awakened
by the wind. How long he had slept
we can only wonder.

But when the Beast awoke he was ravenous,
and filled with fury. He sprung
forward with speed that
was not to be believed. His hunger
could not be satiated,
nor his cunning be fathomed.
Once awakened
his prowl and devastation
continued long after the
wind abated.

His eyes were yellow, no orange, no
red. From his mouth
came stench you could see, it was
black, no grey, no white, and it
lingered.

An army arose to kill the Beast, and
they fought him at every turn.
Only to have him retreat, not in
defeat but in defiance,
and then to reappear
miles away and devour again.

The Beast was given a name, and it
was Thomas.

≳ *Ted Temple*

MY NAME WAS THOMAS

Waking in the morning and looking outside, I saw a fire and it was named Thomas. It reminded me of my time in Vietnam, seeing napalm in action and the aftermath that followed. This fire brought back some of those horrific images. It was frightening and the helplessness of those days in 1967–68 was reignited. This image is a visual of that feeling. My heart goes out to all of those who lost so much in this fire.

Artwork and writing by David Baker
August 8, 1947–May 28, 2018

James Fryhoff
Ojai Police Chief
May 2, 2018

The day the fire started, on that Monday, December 4, 2017, I had worked my regular shift as normal and had just gotten home to Simi Valley, changed out of my uniform, said hi to my family, looked to see what we were having for dinner, got the kids going on homework—all the normal evening stuff—and I get a call from one of my patrol sergeants. All the sergeants have the same number that they use, and I see this number come up and I'm like, *that's never good*. They don't call the chief at home after hours unless something significant is occurring.

My sergeant tells me that there is a fire and that it is in Upper Ojai, that it's a pretty good size and the winds are howling. Because I live far away, I get back in my car and head back towards Ojai. I head to Santa Paula, where the command center is set up at the Santa Paula Community Center.

When I get there, the fire, in a very short period of time, has gained substantial steam. And what I learned when I arrive there, which I did not know when I received the first call, was that there were two separate starts—one that started by Steckel Park, and then separately, one that started up on Koenigstein Road. They ultimately rolled the two fires into one and called it the Thomas Fire, but it had two distinct starts. We immediately got hold of our search and rescue teams so we could do evacuations.

In the Ojai Valley, on every given day, we have five officers and one sergeant assigned to the Valley: three in the unincorporated area and two in the city. This is not a lot of resources when you have to do evacuations and traffic control, so we have a search and rescue team that we use who are all volunteers. They all have regular jobs. On Monday night we were able to pick up the phone and make a call and say we needed them and they were able, in about thirty minutes, to respond and to start emergency notifications in Upper Ojai.

The initial call I got at my home was at 5:45 pm. By the time the evacuations started it was about 7:00 pm. The winds were blowing so heavily, and the fire was growing so rapidly, burning close to an acre a second.

Our number one rule is life safety. If properties are burning, this is certainly not what we wanted, but at the end of the day we were going to use whatever resources we had to get people out of their homes safely. We can always rebuild things, but not people.

While we were doing evacuations door to door in the Upper Ojai area, our Office of Emergency Services ramped up and we started mapping the area and sending out what we call "reverse call directory." We use Everbridge, an emergency alert system for reverse notification. People can get this on their cell phones, home phones, work phones, text messages and email. The more ways that you are signed up for notifications the better. When the fire started the power went out, so if you were relying on a home phone call you may not have gotten it. If you were getting an email and you don't have that on your phone, you're not getting notifications that way either.

For us, the evacuation challenge is multifaceted. When we start doing evacuations, we want to make sure that people are safe, so we need to strategize on many levels: how are we going to communicate with people? What areas are at risk in the near future? How many teams do we need to reach people? And, how are we going to get to them?

Photograph by Jessica Altman-Pollack

With people who will not leave, we ask them for their name and how many people are staying in the home. Because in the event that a house burns down, I want to know how many bodies to look for. We can't force people to leave, but we want to know how many people were there. And, chances are, we are not going back. If we're doing door knocks with a mandatory evacuation, we are probably not going to have the time to come back.

When we evacuate an area, we leave ribbons behind on the property so that there is a mark that someone has been by that house. The ribbons are color-coded to show whether the home is empty or whether people decided to stay. We don't tell people what color we choose because we don't want other people to know who is not home and who is home in terms of looting.

While this initial stage of evacuation was going on, we were still at the command center at the Santa Paula Community Center until about midnight on that first night. Once the amount of equipment arriving became more substantial than the amount that could be housed in the Community Center, we moved to the fairgrounds in Ventura. There was much more room for vehicles and equipment, there were buildings that we had access to, we had places to plug in, and we were able to do all the things we needed to do.

The fairgrounds were also being used as an emergency evacuation center, so we were all converging into the same spot. This was not necessarily problematic, but there were a lot of cars trying to get to the same location at the same time. Because of how fast the fire was moving people were being evacuated who knew nothing about the fire. It was not near them when they went to bed and then, all of a sudden, they are being told to pack up and go, that they had two minutes to get their stuff.

There were some things that made this fire more challenging than others. Number one was the amount of wind that we had. We had 70 mile an hour sustained winds for those first five days. There was no break from the wind. Secondly, it was so late in the season and we hadn't had any rain yet. This was December and we hadn't had our first rain, whereas normally the rain would have come and the undergrowth would have been green and would have slowed the fire a little. In this instance, there wasn't anything to slow this fire down.

What worked in our favor was that the fire department had up-staffed in planning because they knew that there was a wind event coming. They had up-staffed and had pre-positioned equipment and were as prepared as they could be. What we could not do is call for additional resources for a wind event. And so, while we had fire departments from the western half of the United States helping us fight this fire a week into it, at the beginning we did not have these kinds of resources. We had what we had, and we up-staffed as much as we were able.

At the peak of the fire, on day three in Ojai, we went from having five officers patrolling the Valley to having fifty-five officers doing evacuations and managing road closures, and still patrolling the Valley. Normal police calls don't stop just because there is a natural disaster. People don't stop having domestic disputes. People don't stop having heart attacks. People don't stop breaking into things. There is still crime, and police work still needs to be done even while there is a fire all around us. So those five officers that we always have as our base in Ojai were still responsible for handling calls for service unrelated to the fire.

The fire department went through a similar thing, as they still needed some of their staff available for victims of a car crash or for a fire not related to the Thomas Fire. They could not put all their resources on the Thomas Fire.

We found that, during the period of the fire, there was not much looting or crime. Highway 150 to Santa Paula was closed, the 150 to Santa Barbara was closed, and Highway 33 heading up towards Taft was closed. There was only one way in and out of the Valley, and that made it a challenge for anyone thinking about coming up here because they would be stopped by fifty officers. We had the area well saturated.

Once we knew the fire was substantial we opened up the Emergency Operations Center for Ojai here at the police station. The County has an Emergency Operations Center down at the Government Center. Whenever there is a natural disaster that requires more resources than what a small city can cover on their own, the EOC will open up and bring all the resources from the county together. There is somebody representing every shop in this room—someone from Edison and someone from Cal Gas, someone from the Fire Department, from the Sheriff's Department, from Emergency Services, Caltrans... you name it and they are represented. And we all communicate to each other the resources that we have. And all of these departments have relationships with each other that have been nurtured so that during a crisis situation we can all work together in the most cohesive way. When we received a call that transportation was needed to evacuate an elder care facility and move them to another location we were able to send down a trolley to Ventura.

We also had offers from places and businesses that were not part of our governing body. Cavalia, the horse show, connected with us and their horse operators drove their trucks up to Ojai and helped evacuate horses from the Valley. They have all these rigs and all these trucks and all these people trained on corralling horses, and they were able to get the horses out of here in a hurry.

The big wave of the fire was Wednesday night. That it stayed at the

1,500-foot level is really what saved our town. The wind caught it and took it across the top of the Valley at the 1,500-foot plain. Had the wind shifted and burned south instead it could have gone into the Valley, and once it starts burning houses then they just burn.

It burned the north side of the Valley, up above Ojai, and then it moved towards Matilija Canyon. The people who lived there had already been advised and knew they were in a hazardous area and that they were in jeopardy of being cut off very quickly.

After it left the Canyon the fire headed into the National Forest. Once it gets there, the firefighters are not really fighting the fire anymore. Resources can't get to it and the priority of protection of life and structure protection goes down. It is at this time that the firefighters are looking to create natural barriers, looking for ways to facilitate containment.

This fire was an enormous fire. We had deputies that were doing firefighting and deputies that were doing animal rescue. There was a video of a deputy trying to get a pig into his patrol car so he could get it out of the fire.

On the first Friday of the fire, we had our first town hall meeting where we were able to explain where we were currently. There were a lot of rumors going around about the fire and about looting. We spent the weekend following this meeting patrolling Upper Ojai as well as downtown, driving each street and talking to people, and we found that there was not much looting and that the burglary that was occurring was locally contained.

We had townspeople who created a group to patrol the neighborhoods for looting and to communicate with people, in real time, what was happening in each neighborhood and whether their homes were okay. I met with the person who was coordinating this, and we did a sit-down interview that he streamed live on Facebook. I was able to communicate how information got out to the community so that people could get alerts and updates. I was also able to explain that updates are almost always delayed because communications from the ground are told to us, and then relayed to the person listing them online, and only then do they get out to the public. So public safety is equal parts keeping up on the information coming out and common sense, because the information is very fluid. I know there was this perception that information was not quick enough or forthcoming enough, so it is important to understand that there is always an approximate two-hour delay.

One of the things that was really incredible to see was the amount of support for first responders and the amount of support for the community. That people were willing to help each other out. There were neighbors helping neighbors and looking out for one another. For me, it was great to see the community come together. This was a very stressful event and you always wonder how a community will respond, especially because the news is so negative about everything. Because of what is happening to our world you wonder, when you are faced with a disaster, what people will do. In this instance, with this fire, it truly brought out the best in people and the Ojai community was an example of that. To see that interaction and to feel that caring for one another, after twenty-seven years in law enforcement, for me to see that is really important.

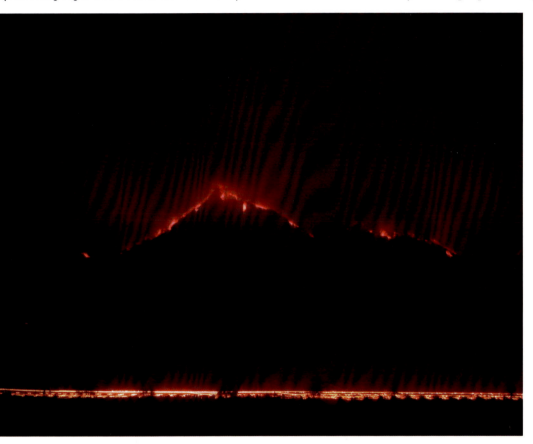

Photograph by Dave May
Lower line of red created by fire engines racing by

Photograph by Didde Heidler Chastain

The fire still surrounds Ojai in parts and ash-filled smoke lingers in the air. My heart aches and I cry for all of those impacted and suffering. Despite their smiles, despite their incredible resilience, despite their best attempts to rise up in gratitude for being alive, underneath is the lurking impact of the trauma we all share.

☙ *Paulette Mahurin*

Left to right: photographs by Johnny Ortez-Tibbels and Erin Parker

John McNeil
Division Fire Chief
May 30, 2018

We had been preparing for some type of fire. We had red flag conditions a day or two ahead of time from the National Weather Service, so we had extra staffing and we were conference calling with other fire agencies, prepping for a potential fire. And sure enough, on Monday night, at 6:30, while I was on my way home from work I heard the initial reporting of a fire in Upper Ojai that started at Steckel Park.

Home is Ojai for me. I work in the El Rio/Camarillo area and I was already in Oak View. It was about a twenty-five minute drive for me to get up to the fire, and in that time I was making phone calls to other chief officers who would potentially take roles managing the fire. Within two to three minutes of that first reporting, the first fire truck was on the scene and reported fifty acres and wind. We knew we were in for a long night.

I arrived on scene and we started putting teams together when we received information that there was another fire off of Koenigstein Road. We all looked at each other as we felt that this new fire could not be related due to the alignment of the wind and where the fires were. I said I'd go take a look at that one, and we decided we would manage it as one fire.

Photograph by Jeffrey Stuteville

I went up to the Koenigstein Fire. It was about a ten or fifteen minute drive, and it couldn't have started in a worse situation. By this time the original fire was ten times the size of the Koenigstein Fire. It threatened Highway 150 going into Santa Paula, the City of Santa Paula and eventually the City of Ventura and was going to be a challenge by itself. This new fire had the same wind trajectory and was threatening all of Upper Ojai and, by the next morning, threatened all of the Ojai Valley. And then it burned around the entire Ojai Valley.

My initial role was to manage this second fire, the Koenigstein Fire. This meant that I was responsible for all the resources that were coming in: fire trucks and helicopters and bulldozers and hand crews; any resource that was going to be used to help put out the fire and save lives was going to be managed by me.

Our initial challenge was to let people know the danger, and get them out of the way of the fire. The evacuations were our top priority, and that was a challenge because the bulk of the threat initially was in the City of Santa Paula, and eventually Ventura, and the phone system was being used to put out those warnings. We did a lot of knocking on doors, and law enforcement used their PA systems to notify the residents in Upper Ojai. We had people in some areas walking around the streets not knowing what to do, and others sitting on their front porch with the fire completely consuming the mountain behind them; they were just giving up. We put a lot of folks on fire trucks and drove them to safety. We did this for the first two days of the fire.

A second challenge was that we couldn't fly helicopters. This is a really good tool for us to use initially to let us see what the threat is. But because it was nighttime and because of the incredible wind conditions and then the smoke conditions, we were unable to get up in the air. This prevented us from really getting a good idea of how big the fire was, exactly where it was, where it was going, and what was threatened.

Monday night the Koenigstein Fire blew through Upper Ojai at the same time that the wind took the Steckel Park Fire through Santa Paula and into Ventura. Sulfur Mountain was the range in between the trajectory of the Koenigstein Fire and the Steckel Park Fire. These two fires came together at the top of Sulfur Mountain, about where that Doppler Radar Station is, on Monday night at approximately 1:00 or 2:00 in the morning.

Ojai Valley School and Meditation Mount were hit early Tuesday morning. Then, at daybreak, the fire went across the 150 at Dennison Grade and threatened the East End of Ojai. The houses along Tower Drive were at high risk so we kept fire trucks and resources available to try and stay out in front of it there. And we finally started to get some additional resources from Santa Barbara, the South Bay and Kern County. The fire came down this side of the Valley Tuesday afternoon.

Also, on Tuesday afternoon and evening, the fire threatened all of the Black Mountain area and Creek Road and all of that side of the Ojai Valley. We lost some houses off of Creek Road Tuesday late afternoon, and then it crossed Creek Road about 7:00 Tuesday evening, burning a structure in a cul-de-sac, sending embers up top and burning a home up there. It is unheard of to be losing structures 24 hours into a fire. At this same time, Tuesday morning, the fire was now through Ventura and had jumped Highway 33. And then Tuesday night it burned along Highway 101 towards Rincon and the Santa Barbara County line. While all this was going on, the fire was also creeping along the other way, near noon on Tuesday, over towards the Thacher School.

Fire has three main influences: fuel, weather and topography. For the Thomas Fire, we'd been in a drought and the fuel had been dried out for six years. We had ridiculous sustained wind and extremely low humidity. But we also have hills and valleys and so the land can actually shelter and affect how the wind acts on the fire. The situation with the Thacher School area is a great example of how topography works. The school was getting sheltered from the mountain range and not getting hit with as much wind, and fire wants to go uphill with the wind, so that's why it slowed down a little bit down where Thacher was. But we knew that once the fire got around the corner and in alignment with the wind, it would race across and threaten the Valley.

That is exactly what happened Wednesday at 5:00 pm. I remember leaving the Thacher School. The smoke overhead was so thick, and all of a sudden you had this phenomenon where the fire breaks from the smoke deck and it intensifies as it gets in alignment with the wind. And it just raced across that whole range. It was crazy. In five hours it got from Thacher all the way across to Highway 33 by Friend's Ranches—which is incredible.

By Wednesday night we had 48 hours in the fire, and we had resources now from the rest of California. We had 150 fire engines up here in the Ojai Valley. At this point the threat to the City of Ventura was over, and the fire was mainly in the remote areas between the Ventura and the Santa Barbara county line. This was the first area of the fire where we were able to get some perimeter control. Until this time we were focusing all our energies on getting people out of harm's way and saving houses.

But here in Ojai, Wednesday night, after running the ridge from Thacher to the 33, the fire jumped the highway at Cozy Dell. The worry was that it was going to go down low with the wind behind it and just blow through the Valley over there. But instead it stayed up high on that mountain, and again, the topography was in our favor because it started high which meant that it backed down and would be slow going down the hill. And that is what happened in Matilija Canyon. It got there Wednesday night and so the residents, if they stayed, would have seen the fire early Thursday morning.

The City of Ojai was quite safe at that point. The probability of a wind turn was very low. The forecast was for those sustained winds to continue in the same direction for the next two weeks. However, we still had some places with a lot of fuel and we decided to back burn these places. A back burn is done because the fire had run on the ridges of the mountains but there was still a lot of unburned fuel that could have threatened the Valley. We did back burns on Black Mountain and again behind Rancho Matilija. With back burns, we light the bottom of the mountain so that the fuel is consumed between the houses and the tops of the mountain. That is about as safe as you can get until the rains come. Normally we use bulldozers to remove the fuel, but we did not have enough resources and so burning was our best choice.

The amount of destruction in such a short period of time was amazing with this fire, and we knew it was not going to let up until the weather let up. We were in red flag conditions for nineteen to twenty days.

When we talk about fires, especially historic fires, we talk about how many acres were burned and how many lives were lost and how many structures were lost. We tend to focus on the negative but there were a ton of successes. When you consider the potential of the Thomas Fire—the scope and intensity of this fire—and when you consider that we evacuated 90,000 people in 24 hours, it's amazing. We put all these people out on the streets in the middle of the night, with traffic signals out because there was no power, and the smoke and wind conditions the way they were. The fact that there weren't more lives lost and injuries with people crashing cars is amazing.

I've been doing this thirty years and I've talked to others who have been doing this just as long. We have the experience and we were ready for this type of fire behavior, but the Thomas Fire was an extraordinary fire. We always make our decisions based on where we project the fire will go, and those projections are usually based on some kind of recall. When there is nothing to recall because you have never been in these specific conditions before, it makes it a little bit more challenging until you figure out what it is about. For example, with the speed of these winds we quickly knew that we had to go out an extra mile each time to get ahead of the fire. And we had to stay at each house that we were defending longer than we normally would otherwise the fire would rekindle. The 70-mile-an-hour winds were acting like a blowtorch and reigniting the structure. So the trucks would stay on these houses, and the fire would progress, and we would have to take a bigger leap to the next place.

We are all going to learn from this about what we need to do to make this better for the next time. We are looking at our weed abatement program and we are looking at how to better prepare homes, whether when they are being built or to retrofit them so that they are not so fuel receptive.

Personally my house in Ojai was safe. We are in the middle of town, down in the flats, and we really had no threat from the fire, so we had all of our friends coming to our home. They were bringing their animals and their kids. I remember coming home at one point—it was Tuesday night, I was up for 36 hours—and I come home for a short time and there are birds in cages, dogs, cats, kids, all over my house. It was crazy, and it was awesome at the same time.

I grew up in this town. I had a lot of connections to the destruction from this fire. It was hard to see all the pain that people were going through. I have been on devastating fires all over the state but not in my hometown. It was very hard, but I see the regrowth. I am in the mountains all the time and see these burned out bushes and see green already starting. It is an amazing natural process. We just want to do it on our own terms and not when we are losing houses.

Photograph by Irasha Pearl Talifero
The Ojai Foundation

We speak in code here now in Ojai when we encounter someone for the first time since the fire, both people we know and those we've never formally met before. We hug and ask, *are you safe?* Which translates to, *do you have a home?*

➢ *Nora Herold*

Clockwise from top left: photographs by Doug Reed, Marc Whitman and Norman Clayton

Ryan Matheson
Ojai Fire Captain
June 1, 2018

We knew about the wind and everyone was on high alert, bringing in extra staff and extra engines and pre-deploying. I knew that there was a chance that our brush rig could be going out, so we had the crew for that.

That Monday night we were notified that there was a brush fire that happened with resources coming from Ventura and Oxnard, because the fire was more towards Santa Paula. Then we heard it was near Thomas Aquinas. I spoke to Chief McNeil, who was driving past the fire station. The fire was already at 50 acres and moving fast and so we loaded up.

We headed through Upper Ojai, all the while listening on the radio that more and more structures were threatened and then we crested the hill and saw that glow from the fire and there was that full moon, the super moon.

We came down into where the fire was and married up with the strike team—four other engines—and we engaged down near Steckel Park where the structures were being threatened. We did that until the second start happened at Koenigstein Road.

Our strike team got moved to Koenigstein, so we wrapped up on the house we were defending and headed off. There were 60 mile an hour sustained winds and the team was trying to get as much intel as we could to figure out what was happening up there and what the game plan was. It was very tricky because we were addressing houses that have structures spaced throughout the hillside. It is an environment that is challenging even on a good day.

We got sent up to protect houses on Quail Trail Road and when we came around the corner the fire was already there. And we're still seeing people in their houses so our immediate concern was evacuation. A lot of people didn't know there was a second start, they just thought there was a fire at Steckel Park and that it was moving towards Ventura. There was a couple that was still waiting for their TV to go back on, they just thought they had lost power and then there was the fire right there.

Photograph by Dave May

We started gathering people and sending them to the Summit School, and I gave the report over the radio that the fire was on Quail Trail and getting ready to hit Fire Station 20. It was probably about five minutes away. Our priority continued to be evacuating as many people as we could and trying to stay in front of this fire. I wish I could tell the exact time of all this, but it was so fast.

Everyone was aware that the fire was in Upper Ojai at this point. Through the night we were just trying to scout out and pick up as many houses as we possibly could by staying in front of the fire. That was the hardest part because we were also trying to deal with the people, telling them they had to leave. Many chose to stay and then when things got really bad everyone went scrambling and we were worried about their safety and were putting them on the engine. This went on through that whole first night and into the next morning.

Being able to read the fire and predict what was going on was a real challenge. I don't think anyone could predict this. We had winds coming out of the east and, at one point, I thought that this is where we were going to gain some ground because east winds will die as they pass the summit as it gets flatter. And though it did kind of let up for a few hours it then did something I never anticipated, it started blowing directly out of the north and then we had basically two fronts coming in.

This fire was nonstop. In between going house to house we were trying to drink as much water as we could and eat as much as we could, and I kept asking my crew *are you good for one more?* because it wasn't ending. Usually you pull into a structure and make your stand and you're in one area, that is your chunk of dirt and you protect it. You're going all out and then it's usually done. And you're on mop up and then other resources come. But this fire kept going and going. Adrenaline wore off and then it's just exhaustion.

I took an ember in my eye and scratched my cornea and I could not see for more than a few seconds at a time. It was painful like someone got a handful of sand and packed it in my eyeballs and I ended up having to go the hospital to get my eyes flushed. My family picked me up from the hospital and I got some sleep but worried about my crew still fighting the fire.

That next day I got medical clearance and ended up being a driver for one of our chiefs through the night and then I came back and worked at the station for four or five days. I ended up switching out with a guy that was assigned to one of our strike teams headed to Montecito. And that was when Cory Iverson died.

I would not have been surprised if we had injuries in that first 24 hours. But Cory passing away… that was the biggest kicker, and ten days later. What was so amazing about the fire in Fillmore at this time—and this is something that I had never seen—this fire backed against the wind. It went up over the hill and it backed down into Fillmore. This fire, it did anything and everything. I had never experienced anything like this. It really put everything in perspective, a firefighter passing away ten days into this thing.

I recently went back to the site where Cory passed away. We were doing training out in Fillmore and we hiked to where he was. We were all familiar with the story and we retraced the steps and a lot of it had all grown back. We had trouble finding the dozer line and you look up the hillside that was just charred with so much destruction and it's all grown.

As firefighters, you want a good assignment which means you want to be out where the fire is. With this fire, there was no such thing as a 'bad assignment' because everywhere was the fire front. It wasn't just Upper Ojai or the Ojai Valley. It was in Santa Paula and Wheeler Canyon and Ventura and Carpinteria and Santa Barbara and Fillmore. And every person, every firefighter, had their own experience. It was the same fire and it was a different firefight for everyone.

You truly couldn't ask for a more perfect storm. Everything lined up. And it wasn't just for that night, this is going back years: the drought, to the relative humidity being as low as it was, the continuous days of extreme Santa Ana winds, to the fuel moisture that was below critical, to where the fire started, the time it started, everything.

We pride ourselves on not losing structures. Our department has a phenomenal record, we have amazing weed abatement and we just don't lose structures. When it started happening around us it was almost surreal. I take it very personally because we lost a lot of homes in this fire. And that is super hard. But I look to the positive that came out of this. As an agency we were stretched to explore new levels, we can see what worked really well and also those things that did not. We can learn from this fire. And I know that for what we did with the resources we had, everyone did a phenomenal job. They gave everything they had.

Photograph by Carolyn Cricca

Photograph by Les Dublin

Photograph by Sharon Butler

JOURNEY THROUGH THE THOMAS FIRE
Julia Thomsen, XplorMor International

I heard news that a fire started between Steckel Park and Thomas Aquinas College. I was concerned, as we've been in drought for a decade, and the winds were very strong. A short time later, I heard mention of a second fire on Koenigstein Road. We have a dear friend who lives off this road. I reached out to her sons to make sure they knew of the fire, and sent out prayers to the universe that all would be well.

Around 11:00 pm I went outside to get some air and stroll off my nervous energy. Our five acres is located down in the river bed of Oak View, surrounded on two sides by wilderness. I walked the driveway and rounded the corner to the front of the house, and was shocked as I looked toward Casitas Springs. There was a bright orange glow coming over the hills. How could this be? The fire started in the back hills of Santa Paula only a few hours ago.

I called my brother Garrick who lives in Ventura. He was aware of the fire and monitoring its progress. At midnight Bryan and I decided to get some sleep. Around 1:30 am there was a pounding on our front door, and alarm bells going off in my mind. It was my brother, his apartment building had been given a mandatory evacuation order. Phones, cable and power were all out in our area, so he wasn't able to contact us. He asked if we could drive back to get more belongings and to help his neighbors evacuate. He took my mother's car and—disoriented in the dark—we scrambled to throw on clothes, find our keys and go.

There were no other cars on Highway 33. With the power out, all was dark. Our headlights showed a thin layer of smoke. It was eerie. I wondered what we were getting ourselves into. I will never forget, as we left Casitas Springs the crests of the hills were on fire all the way from Cañada Larga Road to near The Cross in Ventura. Bryan and I couldn't believe the sight. I wondered if we'd be able to get back to Oak View.

Photograph by Julia Thomsen

We arrived at my brother's at 2:15 am. My brother had already filled the car and decided everything else could be replaced. We stood on his balcony looking at the gruesome sight of one building burning after the other.

Our return drive is etched in my memory. The whole world looked dark except the glowing orange flames on the hillsides. The fire had come down the hills, and was threatening the first line of homes.

We didn't sleep much that night, nor for the next three nights. All lines of communication were down. We had no understanding of what was going on, lots of waiting, not knowing. We pulled out an old radio and tuned in to news, only finding vague information. I kept walking outside to see how close the fire was. Thick smoke and ash filled the air. Face masks were necessary. We kept a change of clothes at the front door. We ran our air purifier.

I noticed a sheriff pulled over in our driveway. He had his hands covering his face as though he was recovering from something he saw or perhaps was tired from no sleep. I waved to get his attention. He noticed and rolled down the window. I don't know how to describe the look that came over his face. He said, *There's nothing we have that can stop the fire on the other side of those hills. You should be prepared to evacuate. How many of you are there? Do you have any livestock or animals to transport?* I let him know we are a family of five, with one cat. He instructed me to get ready to go.

We packed the cars. Around midnight we were outside hosing down our buildings as embers floated in the air. The flames were some distance down river but the winds were so strong that the embers traveled far. We could see the fire burning towards our home with nothing but drought-dried brush in its way. We were close to leaving, but around 3:00 am, the winds shifted and blew the fire away from us. It was a miracle. We all took turns napping.

On Wednesday our power and cable came back on. We had TV and internet, but still no phone. We

filled my days and contributed to my beloved community.

By Wednesday at 4:50 pm, 65,000 acres and 150+ structures had burned with 0% containment. Then, at 6:48 pm, KEYT reported 90,000 acres had burned with 5% containment. We braced ourselves for the coming night as we were told the winds would be strong. We kept the cars packed. With power back on, we had lights and heat to keep us warm. I realized how awful it had been to be in the dark, both without communication and without light.

Around midnight Garrick and I walked up the hill to assess the fire's location. As I looked out toward Lake Casitas, there was fire on the mountain ridge across from Casitas Springs. To the right, I could see fire above the Matilija Canyon area. Those flames must have been at least 100 feet high. In two days we had watched the flames travel almost a full circle around us. All that was missing was around the lake. Johnny Cash's song 'Ring of Fire' hummed in the air, and would be fully realized when the fire circle completed itself.

learned that we had to boil our water before drinking. It was contaminated from the treatment plants being without power. We heard how Upper Ojai had been hit hard and I thought of so many friends in the area, wondering how they were faring. I believe it was this day that I joined the Thomas Fire group on Facebook, which turned out to be a tremendous blessing. I thank its creators. It was through this group that we navigated the coming weeks, made informed decisions and were able to spread valuable information to friends, family and our community. Spreading accurate information became my mission. I posted fire updates daily to this group and on my own page. I included maps and photos where I added more specifics. I posted any breaking news. This is how I

On Thursday, December 7th, National Guard Blackhawk helicopters joined the fight. We watched them repeatedly fly overhead, filling their orange buckets in Lake Casitas and carrying them across the Valley. Their main target was up Maricopa Highway, Matilija Canyon, and the hills across the riverbed from Rice Road, just north of the Highway 150 bridge. I wondered and prayed about friends' homes. Fire broke out again on the ridges above Casitas Springs as well as in the direction of Lake Casitas and toward Ojai. It was spreading beyond our valley toward Santa Barbara County. By Friday evening 143,000 acres and 401 homes had burned. 3,200 firefighters were on site, and the fire was 10% contained.

Photograph by Julia Thomsen

Saturday morning the boil water notice was lifted. The news reported that 5,000 acres burned during the night, and 15% containment was reached; 537 structures were counted as destroyed, with 118 damaged. More out-of-state reinforcements arrived, bringing total fire personnel to 3,993.

The fire entered Santa Barbara County. Governor Jerry Brown arrived in Ventura and a State of Emergency was declared. Though there was a glimmer of hope, as Eric Olsen reported: *The Thomas Fire continues to burn in Los Padres National Forest and around Rancho Matilija area. However, the region is receiving adequate air and ground support. This is the first full day that firefighters are able to fight for containment rather than solely for the protection of life and property. There is no longer a significant threat of spot fires in the City of Ojai. Residences in and around downtown are expected to remain safe.* Eric is based in Washington D.C. as the press secretary and legislative assistant to Congressman John Garamendi. Though our area is not his district, Eric interacted behind the scenes with state and federal agencies to provide updates to locals since Ojai is his hometown.

Saturday, my parents and I went on our first outing since the fire began. We drove to Ojai to restock groceries, face masks and other supplies, and support our local vendors. Our town was vacant. We found the Ojai Valley Baptist Church handing out free N95 masks in front of Vons. As we drove home, we could count seven flare-ups on the hills around us; air support acted quickly and all were controlled. But by late afternoon the northern end of our neighborhood was placed on mandatory evacuation. We wondered if we would be next.

Sunday, December 10th brought the fire back closer to home. Winds reappeared. The 33 was shut down around Rancho Arnaz. The flames had crossed the highway and were in the riverbed. Cars were bumper to bumper down Santa Ana Boulevard. The Blackhawks were in Carpinteria battling the main front. I was concerned, yet as I stood there air support appeared and stopped the fire. By day's end, 230,000 acres and 840 structures were lost. Containment dropped to 10%; 6,000 firefighters were now battling the blazes.

By Monday evening there was only one hot spot visible from our home. It glowed bright over the hills on the other side of Lake Casitas. I could see stars in the sky. I hadn't realized how much I missed them until they were back.

On December 15th, still wearing masks, we finally unpacked the cars, went to the laundromat with our smoky clothes and cleaned house. On the following day, Bryan and I cut rosemary branches from our garden, cleaned off the ash and dropped them off with several pounds of local honey at the Resonance Healing Center in Ojai. They sent us home with several remedies for calming nerves, improving sleep and overall health and well-being. I love Ojai.

On December 18th, Bryan and I drove across the Valley photographing dozens of wonderful 'Thank You' signs that townspeople created for the firefighters and first responders. Creativity and thoughtfulness, joy and love suffused our community. It was heartwarming. We also saw some flare-ups in the hills, accompanied by large cloud plumes, reminders the fire still loomed. That evening KEYT reported 272,000 acres had burned, making the Thomas Fire the second-largest in California history. Containment was at 55%.

Christmas and New Year's came and went. We kept the holidays very low key, just the five of us. We made donations instead of exchanging gifts. January 9th brought more tragedy from the fire as barren hills and heavy rain created severe mudslides in both Ventura and Santa Barbara counties. Lives were lost. It was apparent that our communities would continue to deal with the fire's aftermath for an indefinite period.

However on January 12, 2018, the U.S. Forest Service declared the Thomas Fire 100% contained. At that time it became the largest wildfire in California's recorded history, reportedly burning 281,893 acres or 440 square miles. Over 100,000 residents were evacuated. 8,500 firefighters and fire personnel from 21 states, as far away as Alaska and Florida, joined the fight. Air assistance came from the U.S. Navy and California National Guard. The fire destroyed 1,063 structures, damaged another 280, and cost an estimated $2 billion in damages and firefighting expenses.

I find the stats pretty incomprehensible, even after living through it. Many friends lost so much, yet our community is strong. Rebuilding has begun and life has returned to our Valley. About a month after the fire, Garrick, Bryan and I drove up into Los Padres National Forest. Some areas remained closed, including Rose Valley campground. We could see its remains, and I thought of past campouts and hikes, trips up on Topa Topa. All charred. Through the blackened land, sprouts of bright green were visible.

~~~

The stats I included in my writing were taken from my Facebook posts during the fire. That info mainly came from KEYT news reports and the daily press conferences in Ventura and Santa Barbara. However, I also followed the U.S. Forest Service, VC County Fire Department, VC Sheriff's Office, City of Ventura, County of Santa Barbara, Cal Fire, VC Star, VC Reporter and VC Independent. I am a fact checker so would look at several sources for validity, but took KEYT and news conferences at face value, and if they made corrections, then so did I. I double checked the final stats at CA.gov.

On June 1, 2018, Los Padres National Forest Officials declared the Thomas Fire extinguished, after no hot spots were spotted for more than two months.

Tony McHale
Ojai Fire Captain
April 9, 2018

The Thomas Fire was like nothing we've seen before. Assumptions were blown out of the water. There were unprecedented conditions: dry fuel beds, dead trees, high temperatures, low humidity (1%) and extremely strong and sustained winds with no break. A wind-driven fire is the most unpredictable. And so we were doing things we normally don't do.

We still had a game plan, but the fire moved so quickly and so our locations would immediately change. And then we employed our same tactics, just in this new location. We were always aware of the wind change and the embers flying and jumping our containment lines, and we were constantly making decisions about whether to go directly into the fire from the front or let it burn and come in behind it.

To make these decisions we were also looking at where the fire was. The houses it surrounded, the water we had available, and always the risk to life. There is nothing more precious than life and when the threat to life is so high, as it was in this fire, this is our first priority.

As a firefighter, it's not just courage and it is certainly not an absence of fear. What it is, is defiance. It is the complete belief that we are going to figure this out and we are going to beat this. Because we never stop.

When a fire happens, it is very easy to look at the loss and destruction and to start to value what is lost. And it is easy to become despondent. So it is important to look at the value of what is saved. And to look at the fact that we only lost two people to this fire. For the extent of what this fire was, this is an extraordinary thing. And for this we look to our collective work and to each individual act of heroism, from firefighters and first responders and police officers to the community members—your neighbors. This is what is truly extraordinary about this fire.

FIRE THAT NIGHT

It was not that red wings of flame
raced over hills drained by drought

not that the wind rose up
in mother nature's omen of a roar

not that the sky became tangerine
or the house lost light…

It was the drum of my heart
as my mind foresaw what may come

It was the embodied fear of
knowing I am nothing next to nature.

≽ *Susan Florence*

Photograph by Amun Levy

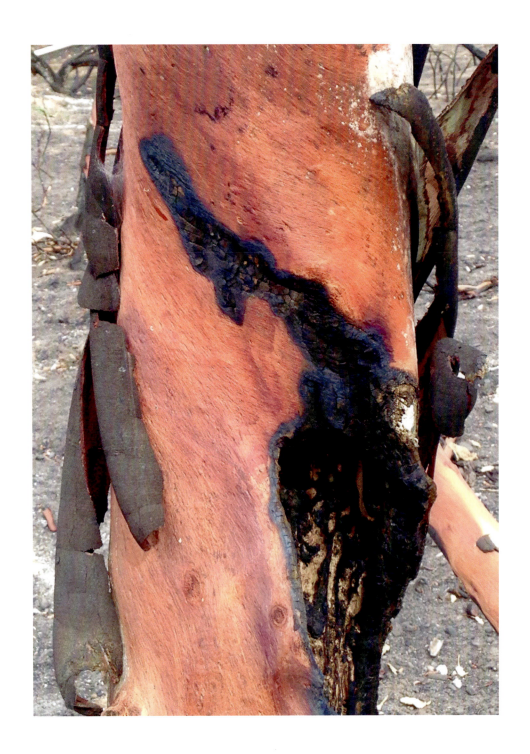

Photograph by Emily Vedder

Photograph by Jeff D. Muth

The Thomas Fire left no life unmoved by its blaze. Both ruthless and benevolent, its transformative presence didn't ask if we were ready to receive it. It just walked right in and brought us to our knees, crossing the ferocity of sudden traumatic change with the gentle grace of unexpected blessings.

Photograph and writing by akka b.
Opposite page: photograph by Jeff D. Muth, looking north from Meiners Oaks

From The Flames

RED THUNDER

I left calmly, with a prayer to accept all as God's will and a small suitcase filled with important files and computer hard drives. Days later, seeing the online fire map drawn through my yard, I felt a lightness, thinking all of my stuff had purged. But the news of twenty-five horses perishing in the Creek Fire in Sylmar brought a powerful vision of Red Thunder. A dense column of white smoke with the sound of chaos stampede as the equines surge to escape and their spirits ascend as ridges of fire blazed in dense darkness.

Artwork and writing by Valerie Freeman
Photograph by Alexa Gerrity

Artwork by Christopher King

The Thomas Fire totally surrounded the Ojai Valley. Although the flames were frightening, at the same time, they gave off the most beautiful light of colors—red, yellow and orange. Our little Valley, known for the lush greens of the citrus and vineyards, became a vision of reds, as if in hell.

Artwork and writing by Gayel Childress

FIRE IN THE CHAPARRAL

Wind smoke fire in the chaparral
Worry smoke fire in the chaparral
Panic smoke fire in the chaparral

Bear paws burned
Mountain lion singed
And where are the condors
Fire in the chaparral

Treebear tent tools all of it
Yurt van cabin in the path
Can't move fast where's the kitty
Fire in the chaparral

So much ash wear the mask
Take it with you what do you do
Gone one night or five
Is the kitty still alive
Fire in the chaparral

≥ *Skip Demuth*

Photograph by Nadia Natali

BRIO DEFINED
Harriette Jump

The night started with a loud bang, then darkness. It was about 6:30, maybe a bit later. Suddenly the air inside smelled of smoke and there was no electricity. I asked my husband, Peter, if he could smell smoke and he said no. But as he stepped out through the sliding glass door, he said, *I see the problem*. He pointed toward Thomas Aquinas College where I could see an orange glow about three miles away. Immediately, I said, *that's not the problem, look at our neighbor's house across the canyon! There's the problem*. I could see 5–10 small fires on the ground in front of my neighbor's house. The fires instantly joined into one fire as winds blowing at 35–80 mph gusts fueled the fire torch diagonally down the canyon in our direction. The Thomas Fire was officially born.

Because the winds were so fierce, I had all three horses in the barn to protect them from flying debris. As we watched the fire sprinting down the canyon, my husband suggested now would be a good time to hook up the trailer. Mind you, this was a brand new trailer that I had never used, let alone hooked up. Somehow, by flashlight, we got the trailer hooked up. The fire department sent up a small truck—not a tanker. We were ordered to leave. My husband told them that we were going to stay. Then the fire department people called the sheriff. Again we were ordered to leave. Again we said no. We were told to just turn the horses loose and get out. At that point, I told the officer that would not happen. They left.

Suddenly, the wind changed direction. I told my husband that now was the time to load the trailer. First out of the barn was my 8-year-old Peruvian Paso mare, Sipapu. She was horrified at what she saw and would not load. I told Peter to give her to me and get the two geldings loaded. Easily done! The problem was it was only a two-horse trailer. Peter drove the rig down our hill to an open field and parked it, all the time with wide veils of embers flying through the air. I've never been so grateful to have purchased a closed trailer as I was that night. Now I'm left with a horse in hand. Peter told me to leave with Sipapu and get out of the smoke. He was rightfully worried about me in the smoke because I have severe asthma and use a nebulizer four times a day for medication.

Do you believe in angels and God's hand on everything? At that very moment, my cell phone rang! It was my veterinarian, Charlie Liskey! He said, *do you need help*? I babbled out, *do I? Yes*! He said, *okay, I'm on the way*. I got in my little Prius, with Sipapu's lead rope coming through the window. Peter asked, *will she do this*? Unknowingly, and not tested, I said, *yes*.

I started down our narrow little one-lane road. Our road is a mile long and flanked by a cliff for half of the way. I remember seeing Sipapu silhouetted against the fire as the embers were sweeping four feet above the road toward us and praying, *please, God, don't let her tail catch on fire*. We began going down the road, little did I know how much debris I would encounter. The first turn we encountered a large storage shed across the road. This was Sipapu's first encounter with the unusual. She stopped. I talked to her and told her, *look, you can figure this out (just don't wait too long)*. I encouraged her forward. Then there were the rocks, then the sheet metal roofing and the rolled sheep fencing. Several times I had to stop the car, get out, explain to Sipapu what we were doing, get back in the car and move on. All the while, fire is burning on both sides of the road. Big trees were down on the road, bushes, more rocks, places where only the car would fit while I asked Sipapu to wait while I passed through first.

All the way down, she kept licking my hand and I cried for the effort she was giving me. Every time I had to stop the car, she would rest her lips on my arm, waiting for me to continue. Then my cell phone rang again. Charlie Liskey called to say they wouldn't let him through the roadblock. Now we were on our own. We continued down and were almost to the main road when we encountered downed power lines. I couldn't take the chance of what

Photograph by Ryan Matheson

the power lines were and we had to back up, uphill, because I couldn't turn around where we were. Visibility was so bad with lots of smoke. We backed an inch at a time until I could turn the car around and go back. I didn't want to be caught in a tight canyon if the fire flared up. We got halfway back up the road when Peter came down to see if we were okay. I told him about the power lines and he went down to check on it. When he drove back up he said *go for it* because it was only telephone lines. At this point, I called Charlie Liskey back. I said, *I need your help, run the roadblock, do whatever you have to, but please come!* He said, *can you make it to the road?* Of course we could. Now, Sipapu and I are on the way back down again. I can still see her beautiful fetlocks so very close to the burning brush. How I prayed that she wouldn't be hurt. This time, we made it through. Charlie Liskey and a friend had brought a stock trailer to meet us.

People who know me understand that Sipapu is more than a horse to me, she is me. D-Ranch people made her. Maidy Dreyfus bred her. Tony Botello trained her. They made Sipapu for a 73-year-old woman with brittle bones, steel rods in both femurs and only a deep abiding lifetime love of horses. Charlie Liskey is Sipapu's vet and he knows that Sipapu is life to me. As we got to the trailer, Charlie took her lead rope to load her. At that point Sipapu said, *I've given you what I can and I'm not going to get in that shiny thing in the middle of a fire.* I asked Charlie's friend to lift me up in the trailer. Then, I asked Sipapu, *please, you've given me so much but just one more. Please, please, I need you to get up here.* She looked at me, then gave a big jump and got in. Charlie, said, *I'm going to take her to my house, what about the two boys?* I told him, *they are in the rig up top.* Charlie asked me if the road was safe. I told him it was really bad. *Okay*, he said, *we are coming back to get them*. And, somehow, they managed that road, and drove my truck and rig out. Charlie Liskey, angel he is, cared for my horses all the time I was in the hospital.

We lost my barn and all contents. I managed to get my Tucker saddle, my old western saddle and a Peruvian trail saddle out. My other Peruvian show saddle and western gear plus lots of serious tack is gone. We lost our flatbed hay trailer, our tractor, fencing, lots of stuff, but we are blessed. We saved our house, horses, dogs and each other. I became quite sick, spending two and a half weeks over the holidays in the hospital with a partially collapsed lung, pulmonary embolisms and some lingering lung problems. Would I do it again? Without a thought. Sipapu never once pulled back, she never broke into a sweat, she acted as if she knew exactly what her job was. We talk about brio. Mostly our show horses are associated with brio, but I would match Sipapu's brio any time. To think, she had never ever been down that road before!

FIRE ASHES PRAYERS

This is an altar to the fierce and gracious fire and the aftermath of deep trust, prayers and benevolence I am continuing to receive and hold.
Fire obliterates both the past and the future.
Ashes are for anointing and awakening.
Prayers hold the matrix of trust.

Artwork and writing by Shahastra Levy

Charlie Whitman
Wildland Fire Fuel Management Technician
National Park Service
June 21, 2018

I have more than the average amount of information about fires because of where I work. Most people were amazed that this place survived and it's often difficult to articulate what the factors were that helped us—why our house would survive and another be destroyed.

I think the number one advantage for our home was that I wasn't surprised. I knew we'd have a fire. Maybe not when, but I knew and so we were prepared. And even though the Koenigstein Fire started five telephone poles above us, we were in a really good place. There is a bare spot between here and where the fire started and a horse pasture even farther up and that helped us a lot. And our property has fire resistant landscaping. All these succulents don't want to burn. We have this green lawn, it doesn't want to burn. We have the swimming pool creating an interruption of fuel. And so we had all these fuel interruptions whereas a lot of people had continuous fuel. For us, the fire would flair up and we would put it out, it would flair up, we would put it out but it was controllable because it was slow, because we had those interruptions in fuel.

Probably the most unusual thing that happened was that the driveway got blocked and we couldn't drive out and so our options were limited. We fought the fire all Monday night. And then early Tuesday morning, at first light, I walked above our land to get a cell signal and I could see flames shooting out of four or five huge homes. The smoke column was so high. The fire was already through Upper Ojai.

My neighbor above us, his house survived as well. He had a water tank that was gravity fed, it didn't rely on electricity and he just opened up the valve and the sprinklers popped up and his house was covered in a shower of water the entire time.

When the fire is raging towards you, you usually need to leave. You need to be prepared before the fire. Turn on your water, close your shutters and leave. Know that what you did to defend your home before a fire is good enough and get yourself to safety. This means that months, years in advance you are accepting the fact that on any day there could be a fire because of the environment you are living in.

This particular fire quickly overwhelmed the capacity of the fire service because of the wind and because two fires started simultaneously so close together. Nothing really could have been done differently in the moment. It's more what we can do in advance, how to manage the landscape, how to slow the fire down, so that more firefighters can get in place. Their job is to save lives and save structures. The more we can do to slow a fire down the faster the firefighters can get to where they are needed, before the fire gets there.

Photograph by Dave May

Slowing down the fire means fire hazard fuel reduction—clearing vegetation away from the structure to reduce the intensity at the surface of the structure—which allows the firefighters to safely protect the home. But it's not as simple as just clearance. It has to be more comprehensive than that. We have to anticipate the fire potential and then we have to mitigate. Many people who lost their homes during this fire had perfect weed abatement. And so it's more than natural fire breaks. It is understanding where to build so that your home is protected from wind. And it's protecting the home with sprinklers and with fireproof roofing and with shutters on your windows.

The question is, who gives the homeowner the information they need to prepare their home? Maybe it's the insurance companies. Maybe they say, *we'll give you a break on your premium if you do the following things to your home.* Maybe they say *we won't insure you unless you do these things to your home and your land.* And they specify the correct exterior sprinklers, the type of roof and siding and window shutters. Maybe this is the industry that has to monitor and oversee this because they have the financial incentive to enforce this. And then they interface with the fire department to ensure that these mitigating systems are in place. When each home is reviewed for weed abatement maybe they are reviewed for those other mitigating items, too. I think we need to create this interface and start this process before these fires that we know will happen, happen. This fire, we will have this fire again.

Top to bottom: Photographs by Kristen Finch and Garth Rose

Artwork by Rick Monzon

PACKING THE CARS

Monday night:
The phone rings, *we're being evacuated, can we come to your house?*
They arrive with kids and dogs and guinea pigs in cardboard boxes.
The grownups are up till 2:00 am when we finally decide
to get some sleep and see
what tomorrow brings.

Tuesday morning:
Everyone in the neighborhood stands in the street,
Trying to guess how far the flames are.
Do we take the antique cello? Ray's kindergarten sculptures?
We start packing the cars.

≽ *Rick Monzon*

Clockwise from top left: photographs by Paul Michael Taylor, Mark Anthony and Leisa Fusco-Foster

Bob Goddard
Full Circle Farm
May 7, 2018

I live in Upper Ojai near The Ojai Foundation. I was in Ventura the day the fire started. Monday night I got home and heard some engines and saw some smoke. Right away I got on the internet and realized the fire was very close, over at Thomas Aquinas.

We started watering things and calling everyone we knew who was in the path of the fire. We knew it was heading west. It's not the first fire we've had here. The last one came through in 1999. That fire was started by kids putting firecrackers in a mailbox. It got very close but didn't burn the property. This was a totally different experience.

We were laying out sprinklers all over the property, particularly on the eastern side where we were most exposed. We were just waiting for things to happen. Most everybody left except for myself and Robert Reddinger and Shaun Walton. We got a fire hose and high-pressure line and we wetted down all around the house. We worked all night to prepare for the fire: getting things wet, picking up anything we could around the houses and making a stash of important papers, cash money and other valuables, medicines and other things and sticking them in our cars.

When the fire was almost here, the fire engines showed up. They headed toward the eastern side of the property. The firefighters liked that spot because it was clear, a defensible zone. When the fire came down the hill it was just wild. I don't know how it didn't burn everything. It was like a living being. There were huge winds blowing. Trees were falling and limbs were flying and embers were going horizontal in the wind. We just said, *we gotta get out of here*. We were afraid that trees would fall down and we would be stuck in the fire. We headed down the road.

Robert was in front of me; he had to stop and move a tree that had fallen across the road. The fire was spreading on all sides of us, like it was following us. The wind was blowing so hard. All that was out here was fire. And Jim Hall, out with his tractor. He's a total hero, a beautiful man. He was driving his tractor, putting out fires on his land. We drove down, and we parked on a broad spot on the road. We put all three of our vehicles together and we sheltered there and watched the fires rage through the fields.

It seemed like the fire might have passed through. We turned around and tried to go back but there were pepper trees and a wooden fence and everything was on fire. It was so smoky, we couldn't even see a foot in front of us. We tried three times. Each time we were turned back by the intense heat and smoke, the lack of visibility. We didn't know what we were driving into. Then we tried to get onto the property from the east side, following the path of the fire. This was

Photograph by Mark Anthony

successful. We could see that the farmhouse had not burned. Even though there was smoke and little fires everywhere, the house was still there. Right away we started putting out fires.

There was some water, but all the pipes had melted in the fire. All we could get were little dribbles on any part of the land. We would take little buckets to one spigot where we could get a little drip out of it, just to the west side of the house, so we were able to make a line across there.

The fire was going through our boneyard, everything was burning. I worked that whole day and into the night. When I finally went to sleep, I woke up and I just started vomiting. I figured it was toxicity from all the smoke and the plastic that was burning and just the stress of it all from not having slept the night before. It was so smoky and there was no water and no power and no phone. There was no way to tell what the fire was doing anywhere else and what was happening.

I decided to get out of there because it was too unhealthy for me but before I left I discovered that we had two water tanks that were full of water and there was one line that came down near the greenhouse that had not burned. The firemen had concentrated here to defend the house above. We had about 15,000 gallons of stored water and gravity feed to one spigot. This was really a blessing because we could gather water in barrels and station it around the land so that when the spot fires needed to be fought there were barrels of water and buckets to work from. It was very fortunate to have all that water supply. The other fortunate thing was we had enough fuel to run the generator to keep our freezers and refrigerators running.

By the afternoon we had everything set up and I went down to Los Angeles to stay with my son Gunnar. Somebody brought over a hyperbaric chamber and I got to use that. I finally felt well enough to go back to The Farm. Most of the fires had been put out but every day there were close calls. It was a lot of just being alert because the fire traveled along the creek bottom below the house and there were embers everywhere and little spot fires. And the oil seeps were still all on fire, putting out toxic smoke.

A lot of people lost their homes. On our driveway there were two homes lost. Everywhere in the Valley there were houses lost and people were really in need of support. Our community, it was amazing how everyone banded together. Trevor did a great thing, devoting energy and resources into setting up the Relief Station at The Summit. The people who own that property were very generous, letting the community commandeer that space beside their store and the whole parking lot. It was really a source of support for the Upper Ojai community—a place for connecting.

Photograph by Conrad Reeder

Artwork by Nancy Gross

ABOUT A BEAR

Oh fire baby
rolling awkwardly in your body
showing something is not right

Still, in your broken bearing there's a clear, sweet light

You accept help, drink water, and
a simple plastic bottle becomes a torch

You light a way for us with your humble, wise life force

We don't get to walk out of this unbroken
We don't get to walk out of this broken only

We don't get to save your crippled form
or hate ourselves for failing

I saw the touch between our worlds as a tableau,
a sort of a different Michelangelo,
a reach across the aisle between beings sharing spaces
and hope, and a call to tend the resources of our globe
more fairly

Worlds collide, there's a
hello in the heart of a goodbye
an open soul in your one unharmed eye

I think I will carry you a long while inside
Fire baby

Nancy Gross

Photograph by Trevor Cox

Artwork by Duane Eells

Ed Bennett
Thacher School
June 22, 2018

Ed, will you investigate the red glow in the sky? I was halfway down Thacher Road, after dinner, when the acting headmaster called me. I looked and there it was. It was about 6:45 Monday evening.

I found out about the two fires and knew that the Koenigstein Fire was the one that would potentially cause a problem for Thacher. We got together at the school, myself and the dean of students, and the director of planning and our CFO and the director of studies and our acting headmaster, as our headmaster was out of town. One of my roles is emergency preparedness and we followed our procedure. You certainly have to be able to adjust to the situation before you, but following the plan was so important. I have been through some serious things as a retired Navy civil engineer officer. I was as proud of being a part of this team at Thacher as being a part of any Navy team. We just clicked.

We organized the buses in case of evacuation. And we communicated with the students what to bring and what to do, to prepare for this possible evacuation. And we sent everyone up to their dorm rooms. When we were done getting everything ready, I began walking up the hill and could see the fire along the ridge line. It was dark and it looked a lot closer than it was. This was around 10:00 pm and we were still assessing the situation. Then we heard about the extent of what had happened at Ojai Valley School. I went into the dean of students' home and said, *we should evacuate*. I don't know that I initiated it or I just verbalized it but we all knew that we would never regret being cautious. We made a call to our headmaster and he was great, saying he trusted us and supported any decision that we made. This was a big thing because he is ultimately responsible for this entire school.

All the parents knew that there was a possibility that we would evacuate. The students were ready. The staff knew that this could happen, but it was really surreal to walk down the hill and come into my office and push that one button that initiates every fire alarm on campus. We have the ability to do mass communication on the campus: 80 to 90-decibel alarms went off and then I sent out texts and emails.

The students were amazing. They were all dressed right and had a single backpack with them and packed the way they were asked to pack. We laugh about this now, but the first to show up and get loaded onto the buses were our seniors and so we put them on the school bus and then the rest of the students showed up and they were put on the nice buses. The seniors were like, *um, this is so not fair, we need the nice bus!* By 1:15 am we had everyone out of the school. Four buses pulled away and also our entire staff and their families. We brought the students to the Cate School in Carpinteria. They are our sister school.

We also evacuated all the horses. We have a relationship with a ranch near Lake Casitas and were able to evacuate 130 horses. We had to bring them back here later in the week when the fire reached there. Richard Winters, the Director of our Horse Program, was amazing. We did not lose one horse.

Once everyone was gone, we started preparing the campus. We made sure all of our water tanks were full and made sure that our sprinklers were on automatic. We didn't have to worry about people flushing toilets and that kind of thing, so we made sure that all the water was going up in the tanks and that the tanks were always full. We did what we could do to make the campus as defendable as possible. We moved cars out of the way so that first responders could access the campus since a lot of our roads are narrow. By 4:00 am most everyone else was off campus.

And then the winds kicked in again. It was sort of funny, it was about 6:00 am. The fire hadn't hit yet. It was still dark and we could see police entering some of our dorms. They were looking for people to tell them to evacuate. We said, *we made that decision five hours ago*.

After that, it became a waiting game. Myself and Jesus Carbajal were on campus and his sons were with us (they work for us part time) and a few others. We went to the observatory with binoculars to watch the fire. Then the first responders started coming onto campus. The first thing we did was make sure that they knew where everything was. The power had come back on and I kept printing out maps of the campus that showed where all the hydrants were and where our tanks were.

The fires hit Thacher at approximately 12:30 Tuesday afternoon. It began to threaten some of our houses and our Gymkhana Field, where our western horse events are held. As the afternoon moved into night, it came into the Carpenter's Orchard, where we have our solar field, and then started hitting closer to campus.

One of the amazing things about the whole thing is we didn't lose any structures. The winds took the roof off of a little tack house out at Carpenter's Orchard and we lost our bees, which was hard, but that was it.

I think it was 10:00 pm Tuesday night that the fire came down on the southeast flank of our school. There was so much smoke and ash. It was horrible, but there was more to come. The fire was circling back around and we knew that it was going to come on us from the north, that it was going to crest the ridge and we were going to see it from that side, too. And then on

Wednesday night at 6:00 pm we began to see the glow through the smoke and the darkness. At this point you're a little numb to it.

It was amazing how quickly everything turned red. It was about 8:00 pm when the on-scene commander says to me, *I want to make sure you guys are ready to go because you may not know it but what you are looking at are 100-foot flames.* I said we were ready, that all my guys had their cars pointed to go out. And then he said, *you're going to need to figure out what you want to save.* At this time there wasn't really much wind, the wind had slowed but there was still enough wind coming down the hills that they couldn't do a back burn. And there was no way that they could defeat this fire with water. We have 1.25 million gallons of water in the tanks and it would have been gone in a matter of minutes and it wouldn't have done anything.

The commander says to me, *we are about 45 minutes away from losing buildings and this fire being in the center of your campus* and so I started circling buildings on the map that I thought should be saved. I chose the most historical buildings on campus. It wasn't that many minutes later that I went down to the command center and I heard, *it's time to rock and roll* and the commander turned to me and said, *Ed, you're going to see something pretty amazing, something maybe you've never seen before* and that's when the air shifted and started flowing up. And now the firefighters were deployed along the edges of our horse program, ready to go. To me, it was incredible patience and courage; they were waiting for the fire. And now they started to back burn. This was like something out of a sci-fi movie, because their flames shot out and everything in the path between the fire's flames and their flames turned black and just dropped. And the fire was out.

The back burns continued around the whole north edge of the campus early into Thursday morning. And then Thursday there was a change of crew. At this time all of the Horn Canyon Trail area was fully engulfed in flames and now we were threatened there.

The fire was coming down Horn Canyon, next to our dorms, and the firefighters tried to back burn but this time it didn't work. The only time I saw anybody excited was the assistant commander who ran up and he said, *Ed, do you have anyone who knows how to run that front-end loader I see that you have* and there were three of us on campus, one being my best backhoe operator. And we cleared a fire break for them with our operator often too close to the fire for my comfort. It took 250,000 gallons of water to douse the fire. We had soot and smoke and a burnt smell, but the actual fire did not touch any of our buildings.

And then, on Friday morning at 9:00 am, we were meeting with the insurance company. And at 10:00 am we started cleanup. We were burned on every side of our campus. From the 1985 fire we learned a lot and that is why we were as prepared as we were, and still I know we can do more. We learned so much from this experience and we are making improvements to how we prepare for a fire.

Going forward we would like to have more water tanks and we would like to have more hydrants and some additional fire sprinkler heads. We have a campus-wide irrigation system that I can control from my phone. I had one of my groundsmen on this system from his home. I told him, *just keep things wet, keep things damp.* A couple of times I would message him some specific areas and he would turn the system on there. One of the first responders asked me if I was turning things on because the water would start running exactly when the flames were showing up in specific locations. It was funny to see the expression on his face. This is a great system and we'd like to add additional sprinklers.

Being in the military, I have experienced a lot of different things but I have never experienced a wildfire like this. I have so much appreciation for the first responders and a much better understanding of what they are really doing. There was this one moment that stands out for me. The fire was up near our observatory and the commander was telling one of his captains to go up there and protect it. The commander said that he'd been up there and it was cleared out, that the building roof is steel, and he told his captain to get up there with his truck and defend that building. And this young guy, he says it looks like a job for two trucks. And the commander says, *I've only got one, I've only got you* and this guy just said, *okay.* And then the commander says this: *and if you get overrun, just lay down, you'll be fine.* And the captain and his team, they just went and did it. The fire raged there most of the night and they were up there the entire time. These men, they are brave.

Photograph by Samuel Tibbels

I left with the feeling that I may not be returning. I packed with the thought of what I can let go of.

⇒ *David Gorospe*

How does one pack, knowing whatever you take may be all that you have left?

⇒ *Nora Herold*

Top to bottom: photographs by Mallory Murphy and Emily Florence

Eric Frye and Carlotta Mastrojanni
May 17, 2018

Eric: Nico had been born at Santa Paula Hospital the morning of December 2nd, and we stayed until the afternoon of the 4th. I remember seeing a wind advisory alert on my phone during the stay, but that was the most we had thought about the weather.

At 3:00 pm we were driving home on the 150 back to Ojai. It was the first time that Nico was in his car seat and I was thinking how beautiful a drive it was. I had an *all is well in the world moment* in my mind. Nico was so fascinated by the fallen leaves and sunny sky, and right at the bend near Thomas Aquinas, Carlotta commented on how beautiful and magical it was.

When we got home to the East End of Ojai the place was still set up for a home birth and it was getting dark fast. It needed a big refresh. I opened up all the doors and windows and cleaned the whole house while Carlotta got into bed for our baby's first night at home. We were finally able to rest!

Then our friend called to say that a fire had started over the mountain, and to leave my phone near the bed in case our area needed to evacuate. We were already triggered by the thought of needing to leave in the middle of the night, after we had rushed to the hospital at midnight three nights previous.

Carlotta: I thought it was a joke and was thinking, *yeah yeah... we don't have to worry about this.*

Eric: And then, soon after midnight, we got the dreaded second call that our friend was on her way over to help us evacuate. Mandatory evacuation.

Carlotta: It was ridiculous. Here I am, having planned for a quiet home birth and peaceful days afterwards. I had labored at home for 40 hours with a birthing pool and then had left for the hospital at 11:00 pm on the night of December 1st in an urgent situation. I ended up having an emergency cesarean. And then we come back home, lie down and have to leave again. I was in complete denial and had no idea what to pack. This was our first child, a newborn baby—what did he need for a 'night away?' And so I literally just packed him one outfit, a pair of socks and one diaper.

That first night we stayed with friends in Oak View. I thought we would be back the next day and could get anything else that we would need for a longer time away. I remember my friend saying that it was cold outside and I said, *no it's fine, we'll be back tomorrow* and we bundled into the car. I don't think Nico was even fully dressed; I wrapped him in my shawl. Our first night at home with our new baby was in someone else's home and bed.

Eric: To me, it felt like the night of a big storm. The power was already out. We had little tea candles everywhere and were in our friends' bedroom. It felt surreal, like we were begrudgingly playing along with a make-believe game.

And then that next morning the fire was coming up from Ventura and the entire Valley began evacuating to Santa Barbara out the 150. Even if only due to the traffic, we knew that we couldn't return to the East End anymore. We met other friends of ours in Santa Barbara, staying at the Villa Rosa Hotel near the beach for two nights.

Carlotta: Eric went out and bought clothes and diapers for Nico. Because of my cesarean I really couldn't move very well. The hotel staff was so sweet and gave us a ground floor suite so I wouldn't have to walk up stairs with the baby.

Eric: But we still found this so hard. I was afraid Nico would make noise in that old hotel and bother other guests, as if we would get kicked out! Survivalist paranoia. There was a huge set of inconveniences on top of the steep learning curve of caring for a baby alone as a couple.

Carlotta: We were in Santa Barbara for two nights, but the air quality was getting worse quickly.

Eric: Thursday morning, the sky was red and the parked car was

Photograph by Emily Florence

covered in white ash, and Santa Barbara was starting to evacuate. We had to go to the pediatric clinic in Santa Paula. Nico had a checkup and Carlotta needed to get her surgery staples out. We really didn't want to go back south and tried to transfer our appointment to a Santa Barbara hospital. But the clinic staff in Santa Paula was so confident, saying that they were open and everything was safe there now. So we started driving back to Santa Paula.

On the way to this appointment the flames were jumping the 101. We later learned they closed the freeway at both ends of the fiery parts, but there were hundreds of us "stuck" in the middle. The police were slowly escorting groups northbound and southbound through this closed stretch, in groups of several hundred cars. But we were completely stopped for minutes. Literally, there was fire everywhere—on the overpass behind us, in the palm trees to our right on the beach, in the grassy median to our left, and across on the northbound side of the 101, on the mountain. The only place there wasn't fire was where there were hundreds of cars ahead of us. People were turning around on the median strip to drive back the other way.

Carlotta: I was in a total panic. Nico was crying. I took him out of the car seat and started nursing him and Eric quietly said, *if we need to go, I'll jump that fence to the beach. You hand Nico to me, and the crowd will help you over the fence.*

Eric: I was ready to abandon ship. We finally got to the 126, which was fine—no flames or anything—and we made it to our appointment. Nico had lost more weight than babies typically lose after birth...

Carlotta: ... and they were worried about him and we freaked out and I started crying.

Eric: That was a turning point. After the clinic appointment we went to our friend's parents' house in Oxnard and we just never left. We stayed there for two weeks with two close friends, Julia and Aaliyah, who were also evacuated from Ojai. They cared for us and we really got the peace, the grounding that Nico needed. We were so grateful for this time. And we were very fortunate to return to a home. Obviously, we didn't know before the fires that this was going to happen but coincidentally—as we planned for our home birth—our friends did a Tibetan Fire Puja in the backyard.

Carlotta: This is a ceremony that helps protect the space by removing any negativity and bringing forth positive blessings for the space.

Eric: We got this blessing thinking it was protecting the space for Nico's healthy birth, but then it ended up also protecting our home. We were the only one of our neighbors with no ash or smoke damage from the fire.

Carlotta: My Vedic friends tell me this was an auspicious moment for Nico to be born. They call him Fire Baby.

Photograph by Debi Otto

Photograph by Mark Anthony

Dave May
May 8, 2018

I got home from an out-of-town trip on Tuesday at about 4:30 in the afternoon, just as the fire was coming down the hill behind our house. I already knew what was going on because two of my friends, who are LA County firefighters, had taken it upon themselves to show up a couple of hours earlier to prepare. They moved yard furniture, trash cans, etc. away from my home, hooked up hoses, wet down some nearby brush behind my neighbor's home and were ready to roll by the time the fire got to the house.

We were lucky they were there. The 'active duty' firefighters were unavailable as they were spread so thin at this early stage. My friends were very helpful and informative. My son and I worked with them for about an hour and a half before they left to protect another home. They spent all week running around providing this volunteer service to many people. Both of them had friends who lost their homes on the evening they helped me.

After they left, my son and I did our best to monitor and control the fire. It wasn't the crazy fire that had happened in Upper Ojai, as it was not as windy and more protected behind my house. We followed my friends' advice to let it burn but not get out of control. We used hoses and shovels (water and dirt) and had moments of craziness and moments of calm. After a few hours a crew and engine from Kern County arrived to help. We stayed on the hill until 11:30 pm and then went into the house. Throughout the night we slept in one-hour intervals staggered on the half hour to keep an eye on the fire. The Kern County guys were out there also. Our neighborhood was the passageway for the fire into the Valley from Upper Ojai but by the morning, with some help from Mother Nature, we had stopped its spread.

The next day was spent putting out smoldering logs and spot fires with a chainsaw and shovels. We inspected many of the other houses on the street and sent messages to let neighbors know they still had homes. The smoke was bad and we melted some tennis shoes, but otherwise we felt relatively safe and calm. That calm feeling was short lived as later that evening we watched the fire take off along the ridge on the north side of the Valley. It was incredible how fast it moved. It was the only time we truly felt threatened as we thought that the authorities would evacuate the whole city and thousands of people would be trying to leave on the one remaining route out of the Valley. This is the only night we left. We jumped in our already packed cars, grabbed two friends in town who had nowhere to go, and evacuated to Ventura.

Early on Thursday morning we returned to our home and to a very different looking Valley. Where we saw a glowing fire on Wednesday night, on Thursday morning we saw a lot of smoke creeping towards our neighborhood from the west along Black Mountain. And then the fire approached Thursday evening, and a whole army of firefighters (various regional departments, Cal Fire, bulldozers, etc.) arrived at our property. It was a great relief to have this support. My son and I got on the roof with hoses and as the fire arrived, I thought we had it licked. Then, much to my surprise,

Photograph by Dave May

the firefighters began firing flares into the brush and natural landscape next to my home. I spent a moment bewildered as I adjusted from a mindset of *fight and stamp out the fire* to *we are setting a fire on purpose*. I had completely misunderstood. Unbeknownst to us, the fire department decided that they were going to do some back burning along Black Mountain. The winds had died down, but they knew if the winds picked back up there would be a problem with all of the fuel on the south side of the Valley. The natural fire had burned to our house on the East End and had crossed over near the Ojai Valley Inn on the west side of town. The idea was to tie these two together with a controlled burn to create a southern fire break between the Santa Paula/Fillmore Valley and the city of Ojai. We spent the next few hours watching another awe inspiring fire right next to our home, standing by with hoses but not actually doing anything as the firefighters had it all under control.

Over the next few days, it was super smoky and we had many small flare-ups from the controlled burn. Again, we would run over with a chainsaw and shovels every time we'd see flames. We would cut off the burning end of logs and bury them in the dirt. We had lots of fire support during this time, mostly in the evenings and throughout the nights. We cooked a couple of dinners for about 25 firefighters. We were feeling lucky and fortunate to be a part of a society where thousands of firefighters leave their families and show up to work in 24-hour shifts for weeks, to save lives and protect people's property.

On Saturday, some administrative firefighters came up to our property. They explained that the controlled burn had not been as complete as they'd hoped. They were concerned about smoldering from the natural and controlled burns and about fire migrating from the Santa Paula/Fillmore Valley. I must have had a depressed look on my face as one of them asked me what was wrong. I told him it would be nice to have a break and explained what we had done and observed over the past two days. I explained that the backside of Black Mountain had burned really well and we walked up the hill to check it out… So I'm talking and he's saying thank you and that he'll take what I'm saying under advisement. He keeps trying to walk away and I keep walking with him—all the way to the top of the hill. Finally he says that he doesn't want to cause more problems than he is solving with another controlled burn but that ultimately they would do the right thing for the safety of the city. When we parted, I was feeling the weight of *here we go again* but much to my surprise and relief, they ultimately decided against the additional burn.

Throughout the week, our decision to ignore the evacuation was based on the advice of our firefighter friends for our particular situation. We had talked about it in advance and they had been up here to confirm our plan. We have a new house, designed with fire in mind and a well maintained and more than required brush clearance. We had our own water supply that has great pressure, a hookup for fire trucks, and lots of hoses and sprinklers that do not rely on the electrical grid. The winds were light in our area from Tuesday through the end of the evacuation period. We had an escape route through an orange grove, packed cars, and we kept our eyes open almost continuously. To reinforce the decision, many of the active firefighters said we were in good shape. The decision to stay was risky, but I'm glad we stayed and I feel that we had an impact on the survival of our home and some nearby property. We learned a lot and will continue to prepare. It was a wild ride and I am glad it's over—at least until the next time.

Photograph by Dave May

Photograph by Jeff D. Muth
Lake Casitas

Photograph by Amy Schneider
Carne Road looking toward Black Mountain

Vina Lustado
Sol Haus Design
June 20, 2018

I was in my East End office on Grand Avenue during the day on Monday. That evening I went home to Oak View, to my tiny house. I first heard about the fire around 6:00 in the evening through Facebook. My husband is with search and rescue, so I called him to ask if he knew about the fire. While I was on the phone with him, he received notification that he was needed. The electricity went out and the internet was gone. I was feeling so disconnected with everything. In the dark, by myself with no communication. A very eerie feeling. I reached out to my landlady on our property—the only person I was able to communicate with. She had another tenant living below the main house. It felt really good to have this community of the three of us. To feel connected to someone else during this dark time.

I live below Saddle Mountain and we were evacuated on Tuesday morning. We went to Nordhoff High School. I was glad to see our Ojai community there. From there, my landmates went to Santa Barbara and I went to my sister's home in Thousand Oaks. I was able to reach my husband, he had been up all night watering down properties to help save houses. The fires were raging in Santa Paula/Upper Ojai, but he was safe. He described having to drive through a huge wall of fire on both sides of the road.

I was at my sister's for a week, on and off. I was grateful I had family and a place to go to during this difficult time. I had a conference that was scheduled for Wednesday up in San Francisco. It felt very strange and challenging to be leaving for this conference while my home and my office were in danger. But for the past four years I have been living minimally in my tiny house and was able to let go of my attachment to material possessions. I left on Tuesday, saying goodbye to my beloved tiny house and my tiny office, not knowing if I would see them again.

I was gone from Tuesday to Sunday, reading about the fire on Facebook—totally unpredictable where the winds would take it. It would die down and then start up again, then jump and spread and then slow down again. And every time I thought it was over it was burning in another direction. Then the fire left Ojai and I came back home. My home was covered in a blanket of ash but still standing. The feeling of relief was indescribable.

I am a longtime advocate of alternative and sustainable housing. Homelessness is not just a statistic. Over 1,000 structures were lost due to the fire. These were homes, offices and workshop spaces where people's livelihoods were made and families were raised. Many dear friends were deeply affected. I see them still struggling after six months, still displaced. The situation for so many is dire and full of despair.

It's crazy because we have all this land. There are so many large structures that occupy so much space and so much of our utilities and energy. Many of them are not even being used because they are second homes. We have so many resources here that we can take advantage of. We can respect the environment and provide housing opportunities to the people who obviously need it while ensuring that we do not overdevelop, that we are in keeping with Ojai and our landscape. Tiny houses are not the only solution for affordable housing, but they are one good solution.

The people here have such a great opportunity to really provide solutions to so many issues that we are facing right now in relation to housing and the environmental crisis. We certainly have some challenges as municipalities all over the country are trying to figure out how to legalize tiny houses. Codes do not exist right now for building and zoning. We have to come up with new codes that combine already existing codes because a tiny house is a hybrid—it's not an RV but it's on wheels, it's not a traditional house but it's built to look like a house, except on a trailer. But our community is full of bright progressive minds with big hearts. Ojai is a perfect place to be a beacon of light for the world.

Photograph by Vina Lustado

MANDATORY EVACUATION

My dear
Danish-Buddhist-Hippie-Boy
What would you think of me
If you could see me
Moving about in a strange,
Somber steadiness

I collect some childhood pictures
Of you in your Boy Scout uniform
Your eyes full of mischief
My cowgirl boots
Your ukulele

I drive through what feels like
A fire cave on the 101
Flaming embers
Slam against our car
Our dog breaks the rules
And moves to the front seat
Shaking so hard that
He is unable to sit

I stay with our friends for days
As a ring of fire
Closes in on our sweet town
And I can't get Johnny Cash's
Song out of my head
And I think—
I should have brought your guitar

I go to bed early one night after
Looking at a fire map
With the false impression
That our home is lost

And I wonder
Would you be upset
Should I have stayed
Should I have brought your ashes

And in that moment
It is as if you are here
In the room
And you are laughing
At the idea of a
Double cremation

And then
I laugh too

And you say—
Isn't it great when
You finally get
The detachment thing?

And I say—
Yes
Yes it is

➤ *Susanna Joslyn Johansen*

Photograph by Julia Thomsen

Photograph by Jeff D. Muth

ALTAR TO THE FIRE GODS II

When I was five, I ran from my first fire. My mom shrieked, *save the valuables!* I saved the vacuum cleaner, a new appliance which for some reason I treasured. Afterwards, I remember sitting in our burnt avocado grove, inhaling the scent, a smell I love to this day. I respect fire. But I've never seen the towering, solar flare-like firestorms like the ones that swirled over Ojai. With Prescott and Santa Rosa, fires have changed. Climate change is real.

Artwork and writing by Martha Moran
Photograph by Mallory Murphy

The fires still burn in front of our eyes, forever burned into our memory. It is that threat that keeps our cars packed and things by the front door ready to grab if the winds shift. Those four words—*if the wind shifts*—I have grown to despise. The wind has subsided but on the ridges it still fights the land in an epic battle. We drive around our town to see where the hot spots are. In the light of day one can see just how close we were to the fire. In the dark of night we are reminded that peace has not yet arrived. Flames still make their presence known and their orange glow says, *I am still here*. And we say, *we are still here too!*

➢ *Cindy Melzer*

The wind came haunting and
ghostlike
murmuring like witches through
the branches.
The devastating forces,
the flames burning.

I took not one picture.
and now,
strangers are candles.

What is burning now?

⇒ *MiMi Alain*

Photograph by Jose Pulido III

Julie Tumamait-Stenslie
June 29, 2018

We live on the west end of Meiners Oaks. When the fire started I looked up and thought, *oh my, another fire in the Upper Valley*, but I didn't worry much about it because it mirrored the many that have happened in my time living in Ojai. We gave some thought to what we would bring if we did have to leave but we weren't planning on it.

But on the third day, as we finished dinner at about 8:00 pm, my daughter walks outside and comes running back in saying, *Mom, the fire is right here, we've got to go*. We looked at our neighborhood and the mountains were ablaze.

We had done a test run earlier that day because we have 14 animals. We have seven cats and three dogs and two rats and then we have two birds, and so we had the two birdcages and all these crates. My husband and I did this test to see how many crates we could fit in my van and how many he could fit in his Prius. And then we started looking at papers and pictures and documents and we pulled out the deed to our house. We only packed for three days, we didn't have room for more because of all the animals.

We didn't know where we were going to go with all our animals. We had gotten a call from a friend who lives in Mission Canyon, out in Santa Barbara, and she said we could come to her. The 150 was closed and so we drove the 101. The fire was on the road all through Rincon and La Conchita. We finally got to our destination and we stayed for three days. We were constantly monitoring the fire and keeping track of the map and at one point my husband said to me, *honey, I think we lost our house*. If you believed the maps—and we did at this point—our neighborhood was encircled in fire. It looked like the fire had come right to our home and my heart sunk.

In all of our travels we collect items that are native made, Zuni and Navajo and Hopi and also the traditional Chimayo Christian mixture of native spirituality. We have the Retablos, which are wooden paintings of saints and they all have a purpose, and then we have Kachinas. And I told my children, when we left, *these are not souvenirs, these have the power of the deities, pray that our house and our neighborhood are protected*. And earlier that day I prayed for the wind to dispel and subdue. I prayed that the fire be allowed to burn as long as it did not harm anything.

We waited a number of hours before we knew if our home was okay. Finally, my brother, who had stayed in Ojai, was able to go by our home. He took a picture to show us that our house was fine. We came back on Saturday.

As a Native American, native to this land, Chumash, I have done a lot of research about my educational, religious and practical life ways, everything that I could find concerning my culture. And after the fire I gave talks about

Photograph by Rhonda Lee

our native beliefs and the benefits of fire. For thousands of years native peoples have known about the power of fire and the benefits to the land. Seeing the plants now, six months later, they are absolutely amazing. The native plants are coming back and they are huge from all the nitrogen and ash.

Along with the importance of the fire creating nutrients for the land, the fire gives us the opportunity for discovery of native sites, burial sites, artifacts and sacred lands. Our tribe has worked on the Refugio oil spill in Gaviota and the Hall Canyon oil spill in Prince Barranca, in Ventura. What I mean by work is that our advocacy is not only social justice but environmental justice and the protection of our cultural resources: our materials, our sacred sites, our artifacts. These are all under the ground. By law, in these kinds of situations when the land is uncovered or disturbed due to natural disasters, Native Americans are called in to be advocates. Not only the natural resources that the biologists are concerned about but also the cultural resources. With the fire there is so much exposed.

I got the call in February to come work on these sites, but we were unable to be included in the jobs. We are not a federally recognized tribe in this region. Because we could not be physically on each site I went to a meeting with CalRecycle and brought over a book of images. I wanted CalRecycle to see what we were looking for. And I started getting calls the next day that items were being found. Finally, we were sponsored by a third party federally recognized tribe, Pomo, from Middletown, CA. They had been on the Napa/Santa Rosa fire and they trained us. We visited 43 properties starting in late April.

Some places were too built up with imported dirt and imported land fill, not our natural soil. But in areas with our native soil, in pristine areas, we found many things. We did not expect that these artifacts would be turned over. They belong to the property owner so most of this is recording. We worked within eight recorded archaeological sites and discovered six undocumented sites in the Upper Valley, and at the west end of Ventura/Santa Barbara county line. We do not say specifically where these sites are. People who are known to loot sites were having a field day because so much was exposed.

Once the debris was removed from a spot, and the landscape was brought back, I could see my relatives as they were when the land was as it was. There is power to this land that has been hidden. Our ancestors knew this. They understood the connection between plants and between rocks, between the animals and ourselves. The fire has exposed this. My hope is that as we rebuild we do not clutter or overrun the land. That we see this natural state and we respect its beauty.

NEW BEGINNING

Fire is a living, breathing creature. It is destructive yet purifying. It is pulsating and primal and indiscriminate. It is necessary yet terrifying. I felt the universe in that fire… the immense, expanding, ceaseless transformation of everything. I have always worshiped fire, marveled at volcanoes and trusted in the process of nature.

I have yet to mourn the perishing of the beautiful forests and chaparral that I love so much. But I trust that this is all part of the process, part of the cleansing and transformation of the Earth. I trust that we will all live to see another day, that the fires bring more warmth and solidarity into the community. That the slate has been cleared for a new beginning.

Photograph and writing by Pamela Luna

PHOTOGRAPH AS ART
⇒ Clay White

The weekend just before the Thomas Fire was incredibly memorable. I had been at John Russell's 80th birthday party, a special evening in that he and his wife have in many ways taken me in like family here in Ojai. The 5th would have marked the beginning of a work trip for me that would have taken me out on the road until right before Christmas. In my work I travel through the United States moving art exhibits from museum to museum. Ironically, because of my work travels, photography had been very much on the forefront of my mind, photographing skylines and landscapes all over the country.

With a morning departure out of Compton on Tuesday, I decided to spend Monday night at a friend's home in Santa Monica. When I arrived, around 10:00 pm, the first words I was greeted with were, *have you heard about this fire that has broken out in Santa Paula?* Then, at 4:00 am, in a dead sleep, I received a phone call from another friend in Ojai who would otherwise never have called at that hour unless the situation was dire. I knew before even looking at the caller ID what the call was about. Come 8:00 am that Tuesday morning I called my drive manager to tell her the situation. Immediately she said, *do what you need to do.* I headed back to Ojai at once.

From Santa Monica I could see the front edge of the smoke line drifting towards me. I took the PCH all the way up to Point Mugu to avoid morning rush traffic on the 405 and 101. I cut back over to the 101 at Las Posas Road, Camarillo, and was now getting some incredible first looks at the smoke plumes building over the Topa Topas. Electronic signs on the 101 North were posting the road closure of Highway 33 into Ojai so I kept driving all the way up to Highway 150 to drive into town the back way. Cars by the hundreds were passing me in the other direction to get towards the coast.

I arrived back home in Meiners Oaks just after noon to a very quiet scene. Being that I was in my 'photograph as art' headspace, after brewing a coffee and checking on the cats—who were wandering around as usual, hunting in the field—I jumped on my girlfriend's red bicycle so I could move around town not being a burden to emergency vehicles while checking out the scene. With a charged cell phone and camera I pedaled up to Nordhoff High School, which was starting to take on the appearance of a storm shelter and infirmary; photographs started to really unfold from this point.

From Nordhoff, I pedaled up to Vons and onto the bike path, shooting photos wherever something jumped out at me, like the serenity of the golf course with the ominous sky behind the Inn, or the tennis courts at Libbey Park. I shot two photos there in an instant, thought of the Ojai tennis tournaments I had watched there over the years, saw their ghosts, then it was into downtown. I felt like I was in a video game of some sort, as if I were living out a removed experience in a parallel universe. It was stunning to experience how desolate Ojai Avenue through the Arcade was. What would normally be a bustling, heavy flowing traffic scene with holiday shoppers on the sidewalks was now, right in front of my eyes, a ghost town.

On my borrowed undersized bicycle I biked as far to the East End as Soule Park and then turned it back around to head five miles back home to Meiners Oaks. Three straight days of unsettling hours and sleep deprived nights unfolded from there. Power was lost for days on end. The flames came as close as about 200 yards from me at its closest call. I watched a row of stately cypress trees go up in flames like Roman candles one after the next with big updrafts of air that sounded rhythmical in their timing, whoosh... whoosh... whoosh... whoosh...

On Tuesday night into the early morning hours of Wednesday, a group of us sat out in the horse pastures for several hours. I remember saying that it seems hard to believe that just 56 hours ago we were all reveling in the joy of my dear friend's 80th birthday. And now here we were watching a mountainside on fire in front of our eyes.

On Thursday morning there was a mandatory evacuation around 3:00 am. I went to sleep an hour or so earlier thinking this was the safest it's felt in 48 hours, only for the winds to shift, and this time the ridge on the west side of Matilija Canyon was going up in flames. On this occasion, due to the direction of the breeze, I could feel the heat from about a mile away, like a warm oven. Something about it actually felt quite soothing, if not certainly strange, with the warmth and the light of the fires illuminating the Valley.

The evacuations were the most disconcerting moments. My approach from the beginning—and my whole reason for returning home when I was due to be out on the road—was to actually be here, at home until the very end, if and when that was going to happen. A good friend of mine lost his home, as did several others who I knew. I was lucky that I only endured close calls. I did look at the possibility of losing everything I had—the most rooted home I've ever lived in with the exception of living under my parents' roof as a kid. Everything that I own is here. All my paintings. If the fire was going to hit my place I was going to watch it. I came to terms that it may burn; I would not have been able to defend my place, but I was going to be there to see it go. I'd like to think I reached a place in my mind where I was okay with whatever outcome God had in store but you can never really know until you've experienced such a loss. Thankfully, I didn't have to go through that. Which makes me hurt all the more for those that did.

Photograph by Clay White

Photograph by Deva Temple
Ecotopia, Matilija Canyon

Jayson Kaufman
Ecotopia
May 4, 2018

I was on the land with Gaviota when we heard the fire had started. We tried to keep up with the information and, when we started to see smoke, drove down the road to monitor the situation. The last time we drove down, a bush on our side of the Canyon caught on fire. We went back to grab our things and we could see the fire coming around the corner. I grabbed my cat and drove to the next houses on the road and everything was ablaze—the houses, the fences, the road. I drove into it for a little bit and it started to get dark and red. I had to turn on the lights and I realized there were too many large fallen rocks for me to drive through, so I turned around and came back to Ecotopia.

The residents near us were hosing down their properties and I put my van down where they were. Everything was on fire; the Canyon was ablaze and the trees were exploding. The fire and the wind were so loud. We couldn't leave, we were stuck in here.

It is amazing that nobody died in the Canyon. The fire came through here so fast. And then it went high. It was raging all around the Canyon and then it just goes up the mountain; up and along the houses to the top of the ridge. And then the next morning it came down on those houses. But this next morning 40 or 50 fire trucks were here. If it hadn't been for these firefighters I am sure many of the houses would have burned.

I stayed in my van that night and the next morning I walked the road back to Ecotopia. There were rocks and burned branches all over the road. On the land small fires were still burning. For the next couple of days we were running around and putting out fires. And then, after a week or so we realized that there were root fires that were still burning.

The fire loves tree roots. The fire will live down in the tree roots underground and stay there and smolder and even a month after the fire we had to dig out and water the roots. It is intense work because the organic matter from the ash and the burning forms a concrete-like substance over the ground. We had to break this up before we could get into where the roots were still burning. We started off with buckets, running to the creek or taking the truck until we were able to get the plumbing going again and were able to spray the roots down. And then we were able get a hold of it a little bit better.

We lost a lot in the fire. We had put a lot of items in the containers—all of our tools, our equipment, and our office supplies and computers—and everything burned. The containers had wood floors. You couldn't see that with all the plants—and the fire burned right under the containers and caught the floors and, with the air coming in, it was a perfect environment for the fire. When I opened the containers there were just piles of ash and metal beams or rafters and shelving that were all twisted and melted. A ladder would be a pile of aluminum. It was art.

We also lost a lot from the land. We were just finishing off this huge planting as we had been working so hard to get this farm going. We lost our electrical house. We lost our shed. We lost our telephone pole. We lost our irrigation system. This was a big hit.

I have not stopped since the fire, and then the flooding came a month later. There was this incredible loud noise and then all this water just dumped in here bringing debris, trees and boulders, and so much mass. After the fire there was still a forest and the flood took it all out. It took the road crew a week to clear mudslides and us several more weeks of digging out on the land. I had seen flooding before and thought I understood it. This was an entirely new thing.

Yet with all of this, I feel that we are blessed. The mud from the flooding mixed with the ash and the clay to create this rich organic matter, and we took this and started to make terraces and elevate the ground. We are paying attention to how we can align ourselves in this environment in a way that allows us not to be damaged to this extent again. And we are planting over 50 trees. We're creating a food forest, so fruit trees, and then some big shade, mothership trees to anchor and protect because these are extreme conditions out here—wind and heat and water. It is going to be incredible.

We had this amazing fundraiser that was such a powerful thing because not only did it help us to get back on our feet, but it also brought in so much love. So many people were supporting us and it helped us clarify that what we are doing on this land is a good thing. We are here to steward this land and people appreciate this.

It is so important in today's society to have natural settings and energies and a natural process with life where people can ground, clear all that stagnant energy and embrace the fluid energies of nature. The garden is the best teacher for us to understand the principles behind the primal force energies that create and sustain life.

This fire was very important. It forced people to question their reality. To look at what was in their hearts and to make changes. It was also incredible for the Earth. This planet sustains life from these burning processes. The organic matter is breaking down and the tons and tons of charcoal and ash, they are neutralizers for our environment, to sustain life—to sustain us. We are part of this regenerative cycle. Mother Earth is saying she wants us here. When we play in her gardens she explodes with joy.

Dan Lang
Matilija Canyon
May 31, 2018

We prepped our house and we went out of the Canyon. We did not have a fire-safe place to climb inside and we had all agreed, as a family, that we would leave. Janis and my daughter-in-law left early, which allowed my son and I to feel that we were not risking our families and we could get the houses ready.

    We put down seven gallons of the fire retardant Barricade and could pump 140 gallons of water per minute for four hours, hosing down our roof and the fire approach area. We knew that our generator would run for four hours and would continue to pump water onto the land until then. By the time the fire reached us, we were out of fuel and pumping no water.

    The fire burned furiously past Ecotopia and went around the bend but then it went up the hill. My preparation may have saved houses because the fire came within two feet of a lot of flammable material but then it stopped at our shop and turned up the hillside. It did not burn through the bottom of the Canyon. It ran above the houses and the next day what really saved us was that there were no strong winds. So when the fire came back down the hillside it took hours and hours and by that time we had so many firefighters here. They protected all the houses in our community.

    Even with all the preparation, it was tough to leave. My brother faced a fire recently in the Klamath River Valley and stayed and made it. He saved his home. He told me, *Dan, I hate to tell you this, but if you don't stay you won't save your home.* Walking away was hard but I didn't question my priorities. I put it in God's hands. If we have our lives, we have everything.

~~~

    We are a Fire Safe Community. We clear a lot out of the Canyon and I believe that is a big part of the reason why we had made a difference on the land. We receive grants for all the hours that we work clearing the land. For every hour that we work we receive an hour of grant time and they send us people to help us. We still have miles to go but we've made miles of improvements.

    We will continue to clear the land. We will have another fire and we have to be prepared. Because it's not an *if* there is another fire, it's a *when*.

Photograph by Nadia Natali
Matilija Canyon

Photograph by Jeff D. Muth
Highway 33, looking towards Sulphur Mountain

BECAUSE THE FIRE CAME

Orange glow
putrid smoke
ash blankets fall.

Blackouts
watered rooftops
neighbors stand together tall.

Evacuation orders
map updates and
brave responders all.

Pets crated, families scrambled
displaced, disheveled, yet bonded together
watch the orange horizon
through nightfall.

Donations overload
commUNITY arises
relief center install.

December calendar planning
black Friday sales
Christmas music
tree decorating
light-adorned rooftops
Christmas pageant rehearsals
now an empty dancehall.
All lost.

Because the fire came.

Amanda Colon Rogers

Left to right: photographs by Clay White and Randy and Cindy Melzer

OUR WORK HAS JUST BEGUN
Marc Whitman

Monday night Julia and I were at a Rotary Christmas dinner when we got word that a fire had broken out at Steckel Park. Soon after, a second fire started on Koenigstein Road, where my mother lives with two of my brothers and a housemate. In our holiday attire, we tried to make it to Upper Ojai to see if we could help but we were blocked at Boccali's. Luckily, my mother's housemate had already evacuated her to town while my brothers stayed to defend the home. The fire came through their property and burned around the house but because my two brothers were there the home was saved.

On this first night we were needed at our Inns in town, the Emerald Iguana and the Blue Iguana. We had several panicked guests and we spent most of the night calming them down and helping them to evacuate. Tuesday and Wednesday were spent securing the Inns for potential fire while getting updates on the progress of the fire from our daughter, Jaide. She was in Hawaii and had access to internet information that we were not able to get.

Wednesday night the fire came. It hit the east edge of our property and a brave crew from the Ventura County Fire Department stood strong. At times it seemed like the Devil was driving the fire onto us, but the winds died down and the fire was held up in the mountains above us. With the help of some of our friends and employees, we spent the next several days clearing more firebreaks and securing our water lines—all the while watching the fire and hearing an eerie roaring through the smoke. I felt it was only time and weather before the fire burned through us. And then on Saturday we experienced two big firestorms.

The first one came through our property at about 8:00 am. It raged down through the 30-year-old chaparral to where the fire department made a stand at the west edge of our yard. This early-morning crew were three very brave firefighters from Bakersfield. They said the only reason they stayed on our property was because of our preparedness. We had firebreaks and gas pumps and lots of water sources (10,000 gallons in tanks connected to our draft hydrant and 100,000 gallons available from our pool/pond). The fire departments used our draft hydrant to pump water through their fire truck.

Julia and I held back at our home. My oldest brother, Charlie, an experienced firefighter, was on hand to advise us as to when to evacuate. Rhett Kemp, also an experienced firefighter, drove down from Glen Ellen and was also on hand as was my son, Nathan, defending his nursery business that he has been building on the property over the last couple of years. We stayed on the property to inform each new fire crew of our water systems and what the previous crew had done to prepare.

After the Bakersfield crew left at noon, and before a new crew arrived from Laguna Beach, a fire flared in the unburnt brush right above our home. With Charlie and Nathan, we cut a line and stopped it in its tracks. The second big firestorm came through at about 2:00 pm from the east. This one was much stronger with big winds behind it. The fire department made a stand at the botanical gardens while we stayed back and put out a few spot fires that flared up due to flying embers.

We know we broke protocol by disobeying the evacuation orders but we believe it helped save our home. As we thanked the last fire crew from Laguna Beach for their brave work, they said that we were the ones responsible for saving everything by being well prepared and on hand. In the end, we are very relieved that all was saved. Still, we are heartbroken by the news of some of our friends losing everything. I think our work has just begun.

Photograph by Marc Whitman

An uninvited monster forced its way upon our beautiful, magical mountain top. Fierce, strong and determined, it trapped us upon the rugged remote top of Koenigstein Road. Evacuation wasn't an option nor was any help from fire crews, just the three of us to somehow keep our animals and ourselves alive. At about hour ten, I walked in every direction around the barn, carrying my little dog, only to stop and realize there was no way out. Walls of flames were moving in upon us and I knew there was no chance for me and my dog. I made the most gut-wrenching decision to open up the barn. The look of calm and confidence my horse Perla gave to me is forever ingrained in my mind. I kissed his nose, walked away and told him he had to go NOW! He bowed his big strong Andalusian neck to me, did a Fabio hair toss of his platinum mane signaling the other two and off they went into the darkness and smoke. The next day Terry spotted the horses and took this mystical photo and texted it to me telling me they had made it! There are no words for the moment I got that text. Once we saw the image of the rearing horse in the flames we knew something unexplainable had been with us that night. The horses worked their way closer and made it back home without a mark on them after a night of running through burning, rocky rugged terrain. My spoiled rotten, pampered, fresh mango eating, bubble wrapped dressage show horse who had never even been out on a trail ride turned into an Andalusian War Horse and saved his herd. I don't remember much after I let them go so I like to think my dog and I survived the incoming flames because Perla guided us out. He knew he had to somehow save his mare because he couldn't imagine life without her.

Photograph by Terry Erickson
Writing by Christie Rice

Photograph by Alexa Gerrity

FIRE. FIRE. FIRE.
Conrad Reeder

At night, I can really see the flames—ominous, chewing away, melting everything in its path. A spiraling flare of tremendous red that looks big from where I sit, miles away, means large things are burning—big trees, maybe big buildings, maybe oil business paraphernalia. Then comes the black smoke, which contains the particles of a hotter fire that's extinguished items of purpose, now some new old purpose.

The fire keeping me awake this dark morning is on the peak of a mountain ridge across the Upper Ojai Valley from where I sit, on a deck that didn't burn in the fire when it came through here. This Valley, my valley, on a plateau that stretches between Ojai Town and Santa Paula for about ten miles, is burned through, so they say; although earlier this night a house across the road that survived the Thomas Fire caught fire when the electricity was restored.

Seems to me the fire gods are having their own say. Little pockets of smoke reveal fires in our yard, and all over the hills, from roots slowly burning which may take weeks. Some smoldering fires are oil seeps, a local item that springs up along fractures in the Earth in this part of the world. They burn a long, long time.

There are many big fires still burning all over Southern California: Thomas, Skirball, Sylmar, Lilac, probably more. Without TV or reliable internet, it's hard to keep up. No rain for months coupled with 70 mph Santa Ana winds lit up the sky around me nine days ago and with little warning. Eric and I with our precious dog, Rocco, drove away fast with flames all around.

The Thomas Fire, my fire, burned up and spewed out everything around my abode: cars (my car), homes, ancient oaks, animals trapped in barns (not my animals), trailers, garages, fences, pictures, tools, golf clubs, books, family heirlooms, Christmas ornaments… but it is the animals trapped in barns that haunt me in my sleep.

By some miracle the house did not burn. Not one window broke in this wood—including the fireplace logs leaning against the house—Victorian. But why not? Maybe the recently watered grass and trees that surround the house, maybe the wind changed or maybe the fire gods didn't need it on their march, doing what they do: burn, burn, burn.

The irony is we create our own disasters by doing what we do, building things where fires have always burned, but where on the planet are there not natural calamities for human-born projects? Floods, tornadoes, hurricanes… Nature runs things on this rock, in case we all forgot. We are merely allowed to reside in the beauty for a very brief span of time.

On this day many of my memories and the comforts of home for a lot of my neighbors now reside in piles of ash, totally unrecognizable from their previous state. The remarkable thing about humans is the desire to mold that dust back into some sort of tangible thing to hold or love, whether it be a structure or a handmade quilt.

This Valley is so unique, so beautiful—I bet they'll all rebuild. Maybe it's easier for me, having already gone through the process of losing my home and precious belongings in some other disaster seven years ago. I survived and my life got better. And if old-timers know, I'm told the fires are done with me, for now. But I keep my mother's quilt nearby just in case we need to run again.

6:00 am. Dawn. The rooster just crowed! I thought he was dead because of his silence these past nine days. I know it's the one before the fire because he has a particular *skrackle-doo*. What a great morning! And anyway, I can't see flames in the daylight.

Photograph by Judy Gabriel

FROM PISMO BEACH
Amber Lennon

The Thomas Fire has us on the run, first to Goleta, now in Pismo. We have been away for four days while the fire rages through the Ojai Valley. Left not knowing whether we would have anything to return to. It was a strange feeling, standing in front of my closet, staring at all my clothes… choosing just a few items. Then scanning the rest of the house for other valuables. *What is important? What do I take? What really matters when it comes down to it? Not much… hardly anything really. My children were safe, other family members also safe.* I end up bringing a small duffle bag, my computer, some documents, a few jewelry items… not much.

I had both restless and heavy, dreamless sleep punctuated by the constant social media checks to see what was happening in my beloved town, Ojai. I realize that there is nowhere else I would rather be; this town, these people, all the problems we face. Those of us who have lived here for many years or feel called to be here for many more, we accept the inherent burdens that are offered from this area. The drought and the fires, the tourism and the crazy rent prices, the hyper-new-age spiritualism. Somehow it is all worth it.

I sit out this fire storm in complete awe and appreciation for the firefighters who are currently risking their lives. Our whole town was surrounded by flames. People have lost everything—I can't imagine. But the power of the images I see on the fire map… our little town completely encircled by fire, mostly untouched. The skill and bravery of the firefighters, coupled with some of that hyper-spiritualistic prayer—*hey, maybe it did something*. I've been spending time envisioning the town of Ojai cradled in my arms. I literally hold my arms in that position, rocking back and forth, as if to comfort and protect everything within my embrace.

Photograph by Debi Otto

REFLECTIONS ON FIRE

Two weeks of chaos. I have few words. The ones that leave my mouth come out feet first and I could care less about turning them around. I have nothing profound to offer. If I am true to myself, I just want silence, a long hot bath and a bed with arms to hold me until I am rested.

Fire gets into everything, that I can tell you. I can also tell you there are two fires: literal and metaphoric. The literal fire chases you out of your home, the metaphoric fire chases you out of your mind. Sometimes the two fires split and take separate paths and you encounter only one or the other, but rarely, if you are in the right place at the right time, you get to encounter both. One works you from the outside, the other works you from within.

You can't run, even though you do. It both precedes you and follows you and just when the flame folds, the smoke rises, the ash falls (and rises and falls and rises) and the flame you thought finally went to sleep, wakes up again. I do not think the fire is going back to sleep. The one in our hills may one day subside, but the fire is here to stay.

It will be here for us in what we lost and what we left and what we didn't leave. It will be here for us in what we want to leave, whether or not we have a home. It will be here for us in exhaustion and in rest, cleaning up all the mess—it will be here for us in anger, connection, joy and grief. Fire is here for us in great relief.

And in flowers.

As in birth and death, this bite will take a long time to chew, but for now I have one more thought: masks.

When your town is caught in a virtual 'ring of fire' the people of the town wear a lot of masks a lot of the time, literal masks. They help protect lungs, the seat of our breath, from the toxins released from attachments that burned. Ironically, there is nothing quite like a fire to dissolve the masks we wear, the metaphoric masks. We 'mask up' when there are toxins in the air and we 'mask down' as they begin to clear. I just can't stop thinking about that—the literal metaphor of everything to do with fire.

We are everything to do with fire.
And I am tired
And I am in bed
And I have nothing to say
And now I am going to sleep
Awake/sleep

⇒ *akka b.*

If I could ever paint something again, I would paint this.

Photograph and writing by Peter Stuart

Photograph by Mark Anthony

FIRE & FLOOD
≈ *Nadia Natali*

The day after our weekend meditation retreat I got word of a major wildfire burning east of Ojai. This was December, and fires aren't supposed to happen then. Nevertheless, this one did, and given the weather report it could easily come our way. The Thomas Fire had started 20 miles away and was advancing north and west in our direction.

It wasn't the first time we had faced a major fire. In 1985 Enrico and two others fought a raging forest fire at Blue Heron Ranch. For the next ten or so years we were spared any major threat, but trees and shrubs grow back, and we knew another fire in the area was possible. When we moved onto our property in 1980, we took to heart the warnings about the high potential for a forest fire, and set out to be well prepared. We put in a 30,000-gallon water reservoir with several fire pumps and many fire hoses. More recently we had added two 5,000-gallon water tanks and sprinkler systems across the property, and two oxygen tanks with masks to use when the air was unbreathable.

The whole South Coast braced for gusty Santa Ana winds, up to 80 miles an hour. Outside I saw columns of smoke rising in the east. Enrico, Javier—who manages our place, and I began to get ready. Enrico showed me how to hold a fire hose. Working the hose was difficult. It was very heavy, hard to open and close, and the stream was intense, dripping all over my hands and feet as the water shot out. I was to cover one side of the house and Enrico the other, while Javier protected the workshop.

That we had survived the 1985 fire like this gave me comfort. Maybe we would this time, too. I began an ongoing dialogue with many people concerned about our welfare. All the telephones were dead, but luckily, I could reach out via the internet to our children and others. I heard that conditions were looking bad and the air quality was dangerous. Many people in Ojai were evacuating.

Two days later, the fire was moving northeast. It split and burned around Ojai, sparing most of the town. After its paths rejoined on the north side, it headed toward Matilija Canyon, and us. For the next three nights Enrico and Javier got up every few hours to check on the fire's progress. Blazes lit up the night sky but were still some distance away.

The next night I decided to drive down canyon, a five-mile curvy road through the mountains, to assess how threatened we were. By then the fire had entered the Canyon and was crawling along the creek's edge and atop the ridges. Strong wind buffeted the car, and I raced home to alert Enrico.

Suddenly the fire brigade arrived—15 trucks and 75 firefighters. We showed them our fire pumps, fire hoses and water reserves and I handed them homemade maps of all the structures. They were very pleased with our preparations. They wanted to wait until the fire reached the top of the ridge closest to the house before beginning to backfire. Burning the fuel below the ridge would reduce the possibility of the fire reaching us. They waited too long, and the fire dropped down to the bottom of the hillside near our homesite.

It was 4:00 on a winter night and it was already dark. At that point the action started, and flares were thrown up the mountainside to start backfires to help direct the flames away from the structures. I stood watching and couldn't help but pull out my iPhone to take photos of the wild blazes devouring the hillside, with some firefighters doing the same. The wind gusts had reached such a high level that the flames were deafening.

The fire burned around us on all sides, completely encircling our 40 acres, echoing the encirclement of Ojai. But we were all right. For a few days I was exhausted and brain-dead, my hands so dry they cracked. Nevertheless, I felt enormously grateful that we had emerged from the fire with little damage. Even though bone-weary, I was exhilarated to have been part of this extraordinary event. Feeling safe now, with so much help and support and knowing that the land around was no longer a fire threat, my nervous system was able to regulate in a beneficial way, knowing I had the ability to act in a crisis. I felt that the experience had been a rare and great privilege.

Photograph by Nadia Natali

~~~

And yes, just four weeks after the Thomas Fire, we heard that a major storm was approaching and was expected to drop up to an inch of rain per hour. After a fire the effect of rainfall can quadruple, one inch of precipitation wreaking the havoc of four inches. The absence of trees, bushes and grasses burned in a fire cause more runoff because organic carbon in the soil is lost, which reduces rainwater absorption and brings flash floods and mudslides. I knew these rains could be a big deal.

On the evening of January 8th, we heard the sound of rain. Early that day I lit a candle for our son Andrei, whom we lost when he tried to ford the river during the devastating 2005 floods 12 years before. All day I listened and waited. I had no idea what to expect. Drizzles began that afternoon and the rain intensified after midnight. Around 4:00 am, an ominous deep roar woke me up, a rumble under the sound of heavy rain.

I have heard the river roar during a storm, but this was different. I woke Enrico, *what's going on? Do you hear that sound?* I worried about Enrico going out in the storm to look around. I wondered if our house would be swept away. After the fire of 1985, we had built berms to prevent that.

An expert assessed our river threat and after looking at the layout of our property explained, *you stop water with water, just like you stop fire with fire.* The Matilija River runs directly down toward our house and then sharply swerves, where it hits a solid rock embankment. It then continues eastward down the Canyon. It would take a fierce, but not impossible, surge of water to change the river's course and hit our home. Given that our land is full of rocks, we had the perfect material to build berms—long, high stone mounds that ran a hundred feet or more. Nine were made, emerging from a central point, looking like the spread fingers of a hand. They provided a succession of barriers, each being the backup of the one above to guide water away from the house.

A half-hour later, Enrico returned with news. The barn was at a low point on our property but far from the river. Sand, water and downed trees had filled up behind the last berm, forcing the water right over it. The debris flow wiped out the barn structure, filled in the arena, and took out all the fences. Gigantic redwood logs, smoothed by tumbling over boulders, lay scattered everywhere.

When I got up to look, I could hear that the river was already receding. It seemed to go down almost as fast as it came up. The parched soil after the five-year drought swallowed the water fast. The rise of the river had spread a quarter-mile from its bed way up to our drive, and downed trees and boulders were strewn everywhere.

Enrico and I walked to the river crossing closest to us. Though the water had dropped quickly, the debris revealed how high it had reached, as if there had been a sea all around. Huge boulders sat where the road had been. The water was low enough that we could walk to the next crossing farther down. That river crossing was still raging, and we knew it would be many days before we could cross.

These two events, fire and flood coming just weeks apart, were humbling. The shift from the fire wipe-out to the flood wipe-out was way more than my mind could grasp. The tangled debris formed an intertwined swamp-scape. There was a kind of beauty in it, and I felt in awe at seeing Nature's volition. I have the utmost respect for her agenda… and her power to regenerate.

Photograph by Nadia Natali

Photograph by Julia Thomsen
Opposite page: photograph by Deva Temple, MESA, Matilija Canyon

Into The Ashes

LOVE'S DISGUISE

Deva Temple

In 2017 three places sacred to me burned: the Columbia River Gorge, a cathedral on the eastern edge of my young adulthood—I grieved the loss of towering trees, tendrils of mist, wildflowers, waterfalls, beauty that will not come again in my lifetime. A month later the Sonoma Fires burned around the place my husband came of age. We watched in horror as our friends and family lost homes, as people died and neighborhoods were leveled. Two months later the Thomas Fire started in Ojai. I glanced at the weather and I knew it would burn everything. My heart imploded.

The first night was insomnia, followed by a morning of panic as we lost touch with my father-in-law who was fighting to save his home in Upper Ojai. Phone lines were down, cell reception spotty. We tried desperately to reach him and to get word of the fire to my mother in Matilija Canyon. Eventually we did hear from both parents. My father-in-law saved his property, suffering only smoke inhalation. My mother evacuated.

While we knew the fate of my husband's family property in the Upper Valley, we would wait a torturous five days to find out the fate of my mother's land. During that time I held conference calls with my family and led prayers that all would be well. Inside I was preparing for a kind of death.

I have become uneasy friends with death. The last few years have been filled with the losses of one and then the other of our long hoped for pregnancies. I held my unborn child in my hand, buried him in the soil, then drenched the dirt with tears. My children died inside of me. Then I turned 40… 41… 42… Nothing.

The loss of everything is something one cannot fathom until all has been lost. I faced into my losses largely alone, in a world uncomfortable with grief. The darkness of 3:00 am became familiar. Countless hours I sat with grief, brewed a pot of tea and held myself feeling the fullness of love when love has nowhere left to go.

When the fire hit, I was as ready as a soul could be and yet the looming loss of my mother's land—the land where I once ran free, donning white curtains in the moonlight, pretending to be a spirit, the land where my feet grew tough from kissing the ground, the land where I learned to name every plant and rock and tree, the land where ancient legends spoke to me and remembrance grew new channels in my being, the land where my biggest wounds were inflicted, where decades later I faced them with fierce love and tender strength and triumphed… The loss of that land would be total, irreplaceable. We would not be permitted to rebuild.

When the fire neared my mother's land I jumped in my car and I drove. I have never made the drive from Oregon to Ojai faster in my life. Still, I knew there was nothing I could do to stop the fire.

When I arrived at my friend's house in Ventura, I was overwhelmed. The stately homes in her neighborhood, decorated for Christmas, threw into contrast the humble land of my mother. It was hard to think that what little she had could be taken and yet those who have so much would celebrate Christmas indoors. *No!,* flooded me. I posted online to ask if I could get into the Canyon and people just laughed. It was an inferno. I tried to sleep, so desperately tired from days of not sleeping, to no avail.

Morning light came, grey and brown and orange. I drove to Ojai, first seeing the destruction in Ventura, The Cross, the hills around the Avenue, then Casitas Springs, already filling with signs of gratitude, and into Ojai where mountains were shaved clean. Smoke still spewed from fires around the Valley.

I blew past the police barricade, waving at the officer on duty with a look that said, *I've got this*. And then I was in the Canyon. It was like a bomb went off. Telephone poles lay strewn about, smoldering. Everywhere was a smoky moonscape. I prepared myself for the worst.

I filmed the devastation as I drove into the Canyon, a place sacred to the Chumash, rightful stewards of this land. I took pictures that I have decided never to share. The homes of our neighbors, burned, struck at my heart. Eventually, I came upon a house unburned, ironically built by my husband's stepfather. The next one also unburned, once belonging to his late mother, Nancy Goddard. Then Jeff and Karen's place, then Ecotopia, the project I was working on when I met my husband. There I found devastation.

I rounded two more corners and was greeted by Dan Lang, his face elated, his arms upraised as if to hug my approaching car. I stopped in the middle of the road and Dan showed me where he had made his stand, where the water he dumped for days turned the fire upward, toward the ridge and around the houses. My mother's land was safe. Everyone in that section of the Canyon was spared.

I laughed and cried and hugged Dan for a while and then continued to see for myself. In every driveway there were at least two fire trucks and ten firefighters. I waved and thanked each of them with tears in my eyes, cognizant that one in three firefighters working the fire were prisoners, people we forget about, who emerge from high walls, barbed wire and the wary eye of armed guards to put their lives on the line for us, perfect strangers.

As I pulled into my mother's driveway I saw first the Tree. We have this ancient oak whose canopy formed the roof of my childhood home. We never were able to build a 'real' house, instead sleeping under countless stars,

cradled by an oak tree so immense that it has grown to form a dome.

Up top I found a dozen or so very tired firefighters taking in the sunrise. One of the captains walked me around, showing how the fire came and how they fought it: a fire line here, much water there, a back burn here… The fire burned to within three feet of my mother's property, a clean line around three sides. A miracle.

Knowing our family's fate did much to soothe me. The personal grief settled away and in its place arose a collective grief. I spent the next two weeks moving around the Valley, touching in with loved ones and finding needs that I could meet.

I spent a lot of time reassuring people that they are entitled to grieve, that loss is loss and that it fills your soul. I sat with people who lost homes, witnessed their disbelief, disorientation and sorrow. There is a way in which we feel we must act when we are bereaved. We want to be stoic, to reassure others that they don't need to grieve for us, that everything is unfolding in perfection, it's for the best, something good will come of this… but when you are in the underworld your job is not to be a cheerleader for the living. When you are in the underworld your job is to be present with the dead.

As I drove out of the Canyon, I spotted a metal chest sitting in the middle of what before the fire had been 20-foot-high vegetation. Curious, I walked over to see what was inside. It was a pile of papers, turned into thin white ash but still intact. I stood for a moment wondering whose life I was witnessing, there in the ash. From that moment the impetus to create this book was born.

Understanding that grief is only love when loss is added, that grief is love looking backward… I knew I could dive into the ashes with all of you, that I could allow myself to be transformed by this confrontation with impermanence. I knew that together we could walk through loss and still, by allowing all our feelings, remain whole. And in this sense of community, bonded by love and grief, I saw the seeds of possibility—the possibility inherent in the human spirit. When the world around us burns, we come together, for this is who we are. It is our nature. It is our birthright. And if we let it, it will be what saves us.

Photograph by Michael Gabriel

Peter Stuart
June 5, 2018

I am sitting outside with a friend, working on the engine of my old sports car. We're facing west and we turn left and can see the fire up on Koenigstein Road. I knew there was a fire in Santa Paula but this fire was new. And within an hour and a half this fire was upon us. I woke up my landlord and she took her horse to Summit School and evacuated.

I lived in a 30-foot yurt, with an outdoor kitchen and living space, an outdoor shower with a claw-foot tub and a second, tiny house. I started watering around my home and my landlord's home. I called everyone I knew. I let the donkey out and hoped he would be okay. And eventually, when I couldn't water anymore, I left. I couldn't take my car with me, I had taken the wheels off to work on it. And so I lost it. And most everything else that I owned. My paintings and my art supplies. Everything.

Sparks were falling like rockets and it was smoky and gloomy and people were running—it was like a war zone. I went into a friend's home, opened the doors, grabbed their dogs and loaded them into my Land Cruiser. And I left Upper Ojai. I got down to the Blue Iguana. And then stayed with the owners at their home.

5:00 am on Tuesday I got up and I'm looking across at Upper Ojai and I know that my residence is probably gone. When the sun rose I drove towards Boccali's Restaurant out on the East End of town. There were police there and I knew they would not let me up so I went to the most eastern end of the Valley. There is a road back near Ojai Valley School and Meditation Mount, and I went up that way but didn't get all the way back to Upper Ojai.

On Wednesday, I'm back at Boccali's and this time I jumped the roadblock, they had moved it to Carne so I went around Reeves, and I was able to drive up the grade. I had heard from neighbors about my home but I had to see it for myself. When I got to Upper Ojai I found the donkey running on its own. The horse was at Summit School. The donkey was wild and it follows the horse everywhere but didn't make it to the school.

It was a weird shock to see where my home had been. I just started taking photographs. My landlord's house was still there, but the barn had burned, and the carport. And my yurt and tiny house. Everything I owned was gone.

I went back and forth a few times. It was hard because the police would not let people up and down the grade so I kept using the road through the East End, through the school. I used to mountain bike there years ago.

Christmas came and friends offered their house on Grand. It is this Zen, mellow space and they offered that I could stay there for two months. I worked their land while I was there. And then Help of Ojai gave me a trailer, which I restored.

I've been in Ojai for 19 years. I used to dream about Ojai. I have traveled the world and have always dreamt about this town. Of all the places that I have been, the only place that stuck with me was Ojai. I kept coming back and then the third time I met my future—now ex—wife and I stayed. I'm planning to leave here soon. To travel. When I do I'll park the trailer at a friend's home. I want to be mobile. Just me and Hank, my dog.

Photograph by Peter Stuart

Photograph by Peter Stuart

Photograph by Clay White

THE NIGHTMARE
Hannah Atkinson

There's a fire near the church, pack whatever you can, we've gotta go. The seriousness and worry in my best friend's voice was an eerie thing to hear. The usually calm, cool and collected woman was in a clear panic and she had every right to be. I poke my head out my trailer door and in the dark was a bright and terrifying glow of red. I went into panic mode. I called my mom, told her about the fire and that I needed to head home to their house immediately, all while collecting everything of value—emotionally and financially—that I could find and shoving them into every nook and cranny of my small Chevy Cruze. In between the frantic packing and pacing I was calling work and my boyfriend, inflicting unnecessary panic on him because what could he do from six hours away?

Having to decide between the things I want and the things I need was surreal but necessary. I didn't need all these dresses. I needed my work clothes. I didn't need all these movies and books. I needed my pictures. I didn't need the Keurig. I threw the last piece into the car, shut the door, took a deep breath and left.

Driving down the grade to my parents' with the ominous glow of the fire in my rearview mirror was torturous. I pulled up to my parents' house, suction cupped myself in my mother's hug, sat with my parents and watched the news. When I'd called my mom at 7:00 pm the Thomas Fire (what they decided to name this beast) had engulfed 50 acres in Upper Ojai. When I got to my parents' house it had reached 500 acres. And not even a half hour later it had made it up to 2,500 acres. The 70 to 80-mile-an-hour winds had fueled this monster into consuming 10,000+ acres by early Tuesday morning. The terror and destruction that swept through Ventura County was like nothing I had ever seen. I fell asleep that night not knowing the extent of the destruction—if I still had a home, the fate of the county.

Tuesday was like waking up realizing that the nightmare you thought you were having is actually the nightmare you are living. Flames were showing up everywhere—Facebook, Instagram, Snapchat—and the news all confirmed. Homes were gone, livelihoods gone, hope gone. My phone rang and it was Jenn, my landlord, hysterical. Her house and my trailer... gone. The air in my body... gone. My dad walked in the house minutes later; he couldn't get to his job site because the whole neighborhood where he worked had been devastated. I broke down in tears as he walked towards me, *What's wrong? Are you okay?... It's gone, Dad, it's all gone. Everything... gone.*

We were in no way out of the woods. The fire was raging on. Staring at the smoke became a hobby in Ojai. Staring at the mountains was all I could seem to do... thinking about the fear in people's hearts in Ventura, and then I saw those flames coming over the mountains. *Here it comes*, I thought. Ojai is a sitting duck, a perfect target for a fire like this, nestled in a valley and just waiting to be destroyed. We packed more into my car, and then packed up my dad's truck, calling my mom at any free moment to keep her updated. She works for the city so she was at the station manning the phones and answering the calls of all the terrified residents. She couldn't leave, she has a town to protect, people to attend to. She finally got home around 5:00 pm and walked into a tense household. I wanted to leave, my brother doesn't, my dad just wants the arguing to stop. My mom and I decide to stay at my uncle's house, a break from the fire for a night, a break from the nightmare. I still didn't sleep—I tried—but I couldn't.

Heading back into Ojai the next morning was depressing. The light of day brought to life the charred mountains and path of the fire, leaving nothing

Photograph by Deva Temple

but smoldering embers as it went. The Valley was quiet, most of its patrons had evacuated the day before, leaving an eerie calm, and blanket of smoke for the ones who decided to stay. I took a shower only to be covered in smoke minutes later.

I had to see the trailer. I had to see it for myself. The drive up Dennison Grade got worse and worse the higher I went; both sides burnt, patches of fire still gnawing at trees and bushes. I turned the corner at the top of the hill and was greeted by black mountains, charred trees, burnt structures… It was quiet, but not the good quiet. The cows I love to see were huddled in the pasture. I smiled. Knowing that they were alive put some joy back into my heart. I made my way towards the house and saw some structures standing, others that had been completely leveled. I fought back tears. It looked like a war zone and Mother Nature had won this one. No questions asked. I turned onto the street that I had been accustomed to returning to for the past three months, and it was just awful. The house they were restoring in front of Jenn's was completely gone. And when I turned into our driveway, my fears were confirmed—nothing. It was all gone. I looked through the rubble for anything that I could salvage and found a piece of a broken plate that I had bought with my best friend Stephanie. An elephant was smiling back at me, a tiny glimpse of happy. I collected myself and headed back down to my parents' home.

Night fell at my parents' on Wednesday. My day had consisted of crying, watching TV, forcing myself to eat, and laying with my dog. My dad popped his head in the door and said, *come on, we are going for a drive*. We headed up by my uncle's house and looked at the mountains on the other side of the Valley. There they were, all in flames. I just thought to myself, *this isn't over, this nightmare isn't over*. Less than two hours later the flames were engulfing the whole mountain, like a wall of fire just coming to take everything we ever loved. My brother and his girlfriend left to head to Santa Barbara, my mom and I headed to my aunt's in Oxnard with the dog, and my dad and uncle stayed. Against our wishes they were going to fight for our home, our memories, our hope. I called my dad about five times that night, and was relieved to hear that the flames had retreated back up the hill, to hear that our home was safe, my family was safe, my hope restored… for now.

My mom and I couldn't wait to get home on Thursday, to hug my dad, to see our pictures get put back on the wall, to start putting our lives back together. The fire was still very much present. I prayed for my little valley, watching as the smoke traveled around like a predator circling its prey. The fear for my home was gone, but the fear for others' homes was very much alive. I checked in on who I could, I reached out to whoever I could get a hold of. I grabbed my mom and we headed out to see things for ourselves. I had never seen an airdrop in person, so watching four helicopters strategically dropping water trying desperately to save

Photograph by Kris Humphries
Highway 150 above Lake Casitas

whatever they could was addicting and incredible. So many homes were saved in the Valley, but not all of them were, an outcome that was sadly inevitable.

Starbucks opened Friday morning. The patrons slowly trickled in, exhausted, grateful to see us, grateful for warm smiles and hot coffee. One of our regulars came in, quietly ordered his coffee and asked how we all were and if all our homes were safe. My manager looks at me and says no. He turns to me, I shake my head. His eyes filled with tears as he walked over to me and gave me a big hug, *I'm so sorry, so sorry, if you need anything don't hesitate to ask*. The day continued on just like that, condolences, hugs, love. Everyone was protective and worried about everyone. We became a big family, all of us, the whole Valley became one. I went home feeling like I was wrapped in a giant hug, like everything was going to be okay. It was. I knew it.

My mom and I headed out that afternoon to try and start to replace things that I lost, finish up Christmas shopping, get back to a sense of normalcy. We had gone to a few stores and then finally made it to the mothership, Target. I was exhausted, mentally, physically and emotionally. I had to get some necessities, shampoo, lotion, soap, things to give to Jenn's kids to try and bring them a little happy in such a dark time.

It became harder and harder walking through the different sections and seeing things I once had and forgot about—the clothes I lost, movies I no longer had. When we made it to the workout section, it hit me, all my workout gear was gone. I lost it, holding onto a pair of gym shorts that were identical to a pair I had just a week ago. All my mom could do was hold me. I just wanted to go home. We checked out, using a gift card my cousin and his wife had given me. I smiled at the cashier, who was beyond nice, and we left.

Slowly I am trying to get it together, trying to be stronger, trying to focus on what I do have and less of what I don't. Yes, sometimes it gets to me. I will think that I am out of tears and then all of a sudden, a hurricane. I hold onto my family tight, force my dog to hug me and am so grateful for the love and generosity of everyone who has helped me. The firefighters, police, paramedics who came from everywhere to help us: Colorado, Oregon, Nebraska, Nevada, just to name a few. My coworkers, patrons, peers—you are all my heroes. I love and am thankful for each and every one of you. Please, if you are hurting, reach out to someone. We are here for you, with open arms we will help in whatever way we can. You are not alone.

Photograph by Rhonda Lee

Heather and Bob Sanders
May 3, 2018

We had neighbors telling us to leave and so we left, but we left too early. We thought we were going overnight and we took nothing with us. We had nothing. Our coats and our cats and cat food and the cat box… and I took this small makeup case, a 1940's Samsonite makeup kit that was my grandmother's, but nothing else. And then we left. We thought we were coming back.

We headed to my brother's off of Poli in Ventura. He called and said to come to his house. The fire was still in Santa Paula at that time. But by the time we got off the freeway at Seaward the fire was already at the top of the hills behind Ventura. We were in our motorhome and we parked facing the hills and watched Ondulando burning, all night.

The fire missed us Monday night, and then the wind changed direction and it came back. Our neighbor had a film of our house at midnight on Monday and you could still see the bedroom windows and the kitchen. And then he pans around and there are the firemen and they are working at the edge of the hill because fire burns up; fire burns up and burns off. But not this fire. You couldn't figure out this fire.

It was like dominos that night. The wind was blowing really hard. We were watching the fire and it was outside Santa Paula and we didn't think it was going to be a problem because we figured it was going towards Santa Paula. We had a fire in the fireplace and I actually did dishes. We weren't worried and then we saw the report of the fire on Koenigstein.

Tuesday night we found out our house and shop had burned. We've been here since '76. We've seen every fire. We've seen fire come right over the top of the hill at 3:00 in the morning. We've seen fire all around us. Many times, though, we knew what direction it was going to go, but this fire, you couldn't know. It skipped. It didn't make sense. There are spots that totally burned and parts that weren't touched. Look at these trees—they didn't burn. The tree that the bird feeder was hanging in is still there, and the bird feeder is still hanging. There's a bag of charcoal sitting on that barbeque over there and it's still there. But our house burned completely.

The house was on a high foundation and it was a long, skinny house. You could stand in the bedroom and look all the way to the side door and there was a big, open kitchen and open living space. We designed it and we built it. I mean we literally built it. We hammered the nails, built up the bricks, everything.

That first day when we finally found out that our house had burned, we weren't in any hurry to come up because what could we do? So, we had a couple of friends that came and took pictures and one friend took a video. And now it's all green but you remember how it was. It looked like a bomb had gone off.

We lived at our friends' house in Ventura. We were in their house and we had just lost everything, and people are singing Christmas carols from boats. It was very strange. We stayed there almost three months. We thought it was going to be a few days or a week, but it ended up being three months by the time we got back here.

Our insurance company was wonderful. I called our agent the night we heard that our house burned down, and she was almost crying. She said we were her third customer saying that they lost their home.

We didn't save much out of the house because I didn't have anybody helping us sift. It's a stucco house, the wood burns and then all the stucco on

Photograph by Heather and Bob Sanders

the chicken wire burns in and so you really can't sift. You can't get much of anything out.

We got a couple of things. I got some pieces of jewelry, and one of them was my mother's gold charm bracelet that my dad had designed that he gave her at Christmas the year they were married. It isn't anything that I probably would wear but it was good to have.

I'm a baker and I lost so much in the kitchen and it was all that old, good stuff. You save good stuff because the new stuff is not as good. I think I can find things, but we lost so much.

I lost my dad's paintings. If I had had another hour, I could have gone to each room. Though really, I would have stayed. It would have been scary and I would have worried about the cats, but we should have stayed. We had seen fire before. And we had never left before. This is the first time in all the years we've been here that we left.

But life goes on. And now we're dealing with it, though there are just too many things to do. And I don't think a lot of people know what so many of us are still dealing with from this fire. We're still figuring out how to rebuild.

We'll build in the same spot. The septic is there and the driveway and all the wiring. And it's a nice spot. We worry about the two big oak trees though—whether we'll need to tear them down or just prune the really burned branches. Oaks have a nice bark that is fire resistant, so we think they will be okay. And we will be okay.

Photograph by Heather and Bob Sanders

Shay Sloan and Brendan Clarke
Co-Directors and Executive Stewardship Circle
The Ojai Foundation
July 3, 2018

Brendan: At the moment when the fire started I was finishing up the last touches on a laundry-to-landscape greywater setup that we had. I had been working on this for a couple of weeks; as of the next day, it was completely gone. We actually heard about the fire when we got a call from a friend of ours who was in the neighborhood who told us there was a small neighborhood fire that was 50 acres. I was cooking dinner down in the Sage House and I stepped outside; half the sky was perfectly still with a nearly full moon and the other half was a huge red cloud of smoke.

Shay: The winds were so strong that before we heard about the fire we were feeling and seeing these really intense—blowing trees down, blowing things down—winds and going outside to try to get a sense of what was happening, closing windows and starting to focus on the impact of the winds with gusts of 80 miles per hour. When we first saw signs of fire we immediately went up to the top corner of the land. We have a very clear lookout from up top and once we got up there we could actually see that this was not a small neighborhood fire. We started to notify the other people who were on the land and some key people on our board and in the community, to make sure they knew, to see if they could find something in the news, to try and get more information about the fire. And we were getting information from listening to the CB radio, hearing the neighbors and the firemen talking about what they were seeing and doing.

Brendan: I literally turned off the stove, got in our work truck and drove up to the top of the land. I was in sandals and a T-shirt; I had just been inside. Shay came up with me along with one other staff member and a former staff member who was visiting. Another staff member and her daughter were off the site at a basketball game in town, and we contacted them as well. And, we made a plan.

We decided we would leave one person at the top of the land to keep watch and the rest of us would change into warmer clothes to be ready for the night and that everyone would take 10 to 15 minutes to pack an exit bag, an evacuation bag. I went down to our home and our stuff was still in boxes—we had only moved here five weeks ago—and so packing was picking up the biggest suitcase I could find and putting it in the truck. And I grabbed the computer bag and one box of files.

Then I came up to the top of the land to basically swap out with Shay and by the time I was back up here—which was not very long—the fire had grown quite a bit and it was then that we saw the second fire starting up on Koenigstein Road. From the vantage point we had and the direction the wind was blowing, the question that I had in my mind was whether that fire had just jumped that distance because the wind was coming so strongly towards us, and because the topography made it seem like the wind could have dropped more

ashes and embers and ignited the back side. If this was the case—and it turned out it was not—then the fire had jumped almost half the distance to us. At that point, once we all gathered up again, we started to make plans for what we were going to do in terms of protecting the Foundation.

Shay: The idea was to take a few moments for each of us to get personally

Photograph by Simone Noble
The Council House

prepared. It was freezing cold and there were those winds. We didn't know how quickly we would need to make a change and so we wanted each of us to have the time to get things together in case we needed to go. And then we would regroup for the Foundation. That whole process was probably an hour for everyone to come back together, to take stock, to see where the fire was and to see what we could do to protect these 36 acres that we steward. It was apparent that the fire was coming towards us. And fast: a football field a second. We had such a phenomenal view. We watched whole hillsides go up. We watched fire creeping as fires are meant to do—in the understory of the oaks. We watched it get blown dramatically up hillsides. And we watched explosions happening. It was amazing to see these different faces of fire, though there was the unknown of what would be the next change. We formed a pretty clear plan of collecting all the propane tanks that we could and watering certain places that we could and doing mitigation strategies that we could so that, as the fire came through, it would hopefully do less damage.

Brendan: There was a particular challenge that arose, having been stewards in one spot on this land for over 40 years we have an enormous collection of archives and photographs and recordings. We quickly got on the phone to some of the elders to ask, if we have to leave, what do you need, what do we take with us? And then we all met up in the office and I said I thought it was time to start watering things down. I tried to turn on the lights, and that's when we discovered the power was out. Since we pump all our water up we couldn't get any pressure without the electricity. We only had a tiny amount of water that was gravity fed back from our tanks and the only thing I was able to water was the Teaching Tree. And then the question became, *what else can we do that would be beneficial to this land without putting us in harm's way?*

Shay: Right around this same time the fire department came and said we had to leave; it was a mandatory evacuation.

Brendan: We politely ignored.

Shay: We continued on watch, and we continued to do what we could do without power and water. We spent considerable time emptying files out of the office, taking boxes of photographs and documents. We loaded up more things for The Ojai Foundation than any of us took personally.

We stayed on the land until about 2:00 in the morning. We had decided on a geographical marker; it was a few hills back from the top of the land and, having watched the pace that the fire was traveling, we all agreed that we would leave when the fire hit this mark and that we would all leave together. That was important to all of us.

As we pulled down the hill away from the land the fire crested Sulfur

Photograph by Simone Noble
The Medicine Wheel

Mountain. We hadn't been able to see what was coming from that direction until we left the Foundation. We were driving down the hill and the entire hillside was backlit in flames. We went to town, and we thanked each other for what we had done, and we all went to stay with different friends. And the journey went on from there, changing every day. On Tuesday we needed to evacuate the place we were staying in town, on the East End. And on Wednesday we came back to the land.

Brendan: When we drove down the hill from the Foundation, at 2:00 am, the firefighters were blocking our road. They had bulldozers and our understanding was that they were going to try and make a fire line. When we showed up they were so surprised to see us. The Ojai Foundation is set up with a scenic protection; everything we build is basically not visible from the road plus we had lost power so from their vantage point the place was empty. The only thing they eventually saw were headlights coming down the hill towards them.

Shay: We left at 2:00 am and our understanding was that the fire moved through the land between 6:00 and 7:00 am. It consumed our entire acreage so we assumed that it hit the land from several different directions. We got back here on Wednesday and spent our first hours that day putting out small fires and making firebreaks, so the fire creep could not continue underground. There was a lot of ground creep still happening, fire was burning in the embers and in the ground cover, and there were live fires all over the land, but the main body of fire had passed through. It was completely burnt. I mean phenomenally, bizarrely, forever changed.

The Gateway (welcoming place), and the office, a couple of restrooms, the Council House, kivas, one other meeting space and our shrines all survived the fire. Nearly every other structure on the land was taken: 27 structures were lost to the fire. Yurts, domes and smaller buildings that were for accommodations and the restrooms, our kitchen, our pottery studio and so much more…

Brendan: … and our staff residence.

Shay: The six of us who were on the land during the fire all lost everything that we did not take with us—our things and our home. We came back, and it was like a reverse treasure hunt—we would go to one building and see what happened, and then to another place to see. And we were trying to take mental stock of what was gone and of what remained and how we could mitigate any further loss.

Brendan: When we were able to arrive back on the land there were small fires still happening everywhere, including burning logs that were near propane tanks,

Photograph by Simone Noble
The Yurt

not a great scene, and we started looking around for what we could use to put the fires out because all of our tools had burned. We had this one moment where someone had just the head of a shovel—the handle had burnt—and was shoveling dirt onto a fire. We had to take a moment to evaluate. Even with the fires still burning it was calm enough that we were able to take stock and look around. And so much was gone. Black ash…

Shay: … and char. And so many burned animals. Burned rabbits and injured birds and squirrels and so many little creatures.

Brendan: One of the first things we did was fill water bowls for the animals.

Shay: Even before we came back to the land, a few others had made it up to the Foundation and we found out on Tuesday afternoon that the fire had burned through, and that what had been damaged was visible and could be taken stock of. Our home was gone. We had that day to process this before we came back to the land. And one of the truths for us is that our personal loss has been situated in the loss for the Foundation, which has been situated in the loss for the community. I would say we've never dwelled too much on any one of the losses in isolation but that all of them coexist for us. I feel that there have been huge gifts in that, to not just be in me and my story and my loss but in the awareness of the scale of change that is happening in the region and also in the world.

Brendan: One of the biggest reasons to come back to the land so quickly, outside of our own need to know, was because this place is important to so many people. The rumor mill was flying about what happened and we needed to get here and make an assessment and make a public announcement to our community.

Shay: On the morning we got back, one of our elders who lives up on Sulfur Mountain Road and has been involved with the Foundation since its early days, came down to walk the land with us. Her husband, too. We also had our board co-chair and two firefighters—the current and previous Santa Barbara fire chiefs. We got to walk the land with the fire experts and really understand what we were seeing. And we got to stand with an elder who had planted the trees that were now burned and we were able to see her loss in the context of our own loss.

Brendan: We have been really working hard to understand what happened with our structures here. The Foundation has been a place that is working with the principles of sustainability and regenerative design and alternative building methods, earth building/natural building. Our natural buildings did phenomenally well when compared to the conventional structures that are on the land. We had some that burned inside and out and are still standing, and we have other, conventionally built, structures that were fully to fire code, and they are gone. It is important to document and understand and to share that story as we look at our region, and I would say a our world, that is facing a next level of intensity of these kinds of elemental forces and fires and to ask, *what, if anything, can we contribute to this story?*

Brendan: One of the folks who we connected with shortly after the fire spoke with us about the nature of fire and the particular kind of transformation it allows for, which is this capacity to merge different elements—melting things together, which we could see physically on the land: melted glass had merged with melted plastic and then with wood. And this notion of coalescence, I felt that happening on the human level in the Ojai community. We were, in essence, pushed off this hill and then brought into the community in a very strong way, in our roles in The Ojai Foundation, and as people. And we were caught by our global community of friends in an incredible way. I felt very well held in the midst of a tremendously large transformation and transition. And the practices that I have learned from places like this—like council circle—were serving me

Photograph by Simone Noble
The Ancestors Shrine

in these times I really needed them. These practices were being put to test in the real thing, and they were serving well. I feel like this fire has brought gifts. It certainly is not that it is all good; we are not going to bypass the pain or the grief or the loss and suffering. It is not all rosy, but it has brought with it, for me, a tremendous number of gifts alongside the destruction. To be able to hold these in balance has been one of the creative tensions in the wake of the fire.

One of these unexpected gifts for me is that I have spent a lot of my life making decisions based on trying to respond, in the ways that I can, to the realities of climate change. Mostly that has been something that is 'out there.' But now, with the loss of home, quite literally, we are asked to find home in a very different sense. And to rest into community in a deeper way. And to land more fully in the story of our times, which, for me is, at least in part, that of climate change. I consider us, with the loss of home, as climate refugees and I don't think it's any fluke that the fires are getting bigger and stronger and the question is, *what is our response now, knowing that this is a global issue? What can we do here, and how can we not ignore the pattern and the relationship of the different places and the people and the flows of some of these large forces that are at play?* To come home to this story in an unexpected way has been one of the hardest and most beautiful parts of this fire… to actually feel this, day to day. There is no going back.

Shay: From that first moment of seeing the fire and the scale of the fire we started a process of triage: what is essential, what's needed now? And that has continued and is still continuing today. We are still in a deep process of recovery for ourselves and the land. We are still clearing burnt trees and brush and discovering things that we didn't know on an infrastructure level. People keep asking what we will rebuild and when we will reopen. And we don't fully know. And these are good questions. It is one step at a time. I feel these tremendous gifts that Brendan is naming. And I feel the challenge and the ongoing need for good pacing and good balance to regroup, and not only in our personal lives but also for the community. There has been so much loss for those that have invested their life's work in The Ojai Foundation and might not find some of that work here anymore or might find that the work has changed. We will continue to steward this deep and profound process of change and transformation that is still rippling and affecting the lives of hundreds, maybe thousands of people, all people who are deeply tied to the Foundation. I feel deeply responsible and also deeply humbled.

Photograph by Simone Noble
The Teaching Tree

The air had a gritty layer
that sat in place
and whirled ash and dirt.
Life was turned upside down

❧ *Brenton Butler*

The Thomas Fire had a way of revealing images of old cars
and trucks that went off the roads and highways in the
Valley and have been hidden for decades.

❧ *Christina Fortney*

*Left to right: photographs by Barbara Muska
and Grant Fortney*

Corinna Bloom, Tim Hall and Art Durand
Meditation Mount
June 25, 2018

Corinna: I was down in town and at 8:00 pm I came back up to the Mount. I had sent all the resident staff members a message that there was a fire which had grown to 500 acres. At first, I thought it was okay, but then we could see the glow over the hill and we knew that it was serious. We had a meeting on the parking lot to briefly discuss the plan—Art would pull out the fire hose and Tim would begin drenching the hillsides with water, and the rest of us would collect our essential belongings into our cars. At 11:00 pm there was a mandatory evacuation. Everyone left except Art and Tim. I was really concerned about them staying because I knew that if the fire came it would burn all the way around and we only have one exit road up here, and I also knew that Art—not unlike any firefighter—is willing to get hurt for the cause.

Tim: At night we irrigate so I was out there, and I see a glow to the east. It was about 8:00 pm on Monday night. It's December so it's totally dark at that time. The glow was pretty significant and there was a lot of wind. Art is trained as a firefighter and I was in the Navy and so we didn't have to talk about much. We just went out there and he started getting the fire hoses out and I went around and turned on the irrigation, especially on the east side since that is where the fire would approach. It is the most vulnerable because we have an old wooden shed that would have gone up like tinder and we have the workshop that would have easily burned—it had a wooden frame. And then there was the garage and then Art's house and then mine, and finally, our main building. This fire would have burned right through all of this if we had allowed it to get to that first building.

Art: We fought the fire early Tuesday morning. We had been preparing all night and listening to the scanner and we could hear that the fire was in Ventura and that the wind was very bad and that the helicopters could not be used. We're following all this, and it's crystal clear that the fire is coming. It's about 6:15 in the morning and the night sky is clear above us and then by 6:50 it's dawn and we are covered in smoke and we are in it.

Tim: There were two or three fire trucks at Ojai Valley School. It hit them first at the highest part of their land, where the girls' dorm and the science building were. We watched it leave OVS and head down the hill and then back up to us. The place was soaked by the time the fire reached us. Earlier in the morning, at around 3:00 am, a fire chief had come up and asked who was here and we said, it's just us. He said we needed more resources and he would send some, and then we never saw anyone. We know they showed up afterwards because there were spray marks on the outside of the building and parts of some of our wooden structures had been kicked away where they had burned. But while we were fighting the fire, we were here alone.

Art: The county was just completely overwhelmed because of the wind. We were listening to the scanner all night and they were begging for air support. They were very calm and professional, still asking for air support but it was too windy.

Corinna: Two of us went over to the Ojai Retreat and could see the fire from there, up on the hill. I slept all of an hour that night and kept going outside to check on Art and Tim. When I drove back to the Mount at 3:00 am, they were already haggard. And then in the early morning I came by again, the police weren't there yet to stop people. I could see the fire coming over the crest, and from where I was at the Ojai Retreat it looked like the

Photograph by Art Durand
Remnants of the Tree House—'Spirit Transcending Destruction'

whole mountain was burning, and so I drove back over to see what it was like. I had been texting Art and he kept reassuring me that they were okay, but I had to come over to see for myself.

Art: We watched the fire come around and we were able to fight the flames because we had a lot of water. It comes off the tanks up here, we had hydrant pressure and one and a half inch hoses.

Tim: There was a spot fire in an odd place that could have taken everything out if it had been able to grow, we ran over there with the hose and the wind was so loud we had to yell at each other even though we were standing right next to each other. And all of a sudden, the crown of the tree breaks and crashes down right by us. It came down and it knocked over another tree. And we just kept fighting the fire. We didn't even look up. We heard it cracking, we couldn't see much and we had stuff to do.

Art: Our last stand was at the house that we ended up losing. We were right there at the end of the parking lot and the wind was blowing so hard and it turned our stream back onto us. That was how strong the wind was. It was nice because it was wet and we were hot from all the smoke but it was intense and so we had to stop. And we knew we had to leave.

Tim: If we could have gotten around the side of the fire we might have been able to save it, but we didn't have enough hose to do that. There would be embers flying and we started running after them and putting out any flare-ups and then it just got too windy—the wind was too great and was full of smoke and ash and embers and dirt and leaves. We had these cheap masks but our eyes were exposed and it soon became too much. There was nothing we could do. It was time to leave. When we drove out we were surrounded on both sides of the road by fire. It didn't seem hard to leave. There was no question to stay when we stayed and to leave when it was time to leave.

Corinna: For Art it was hard to leave. He wanted to save that house, he had promised our friends that he would…

Tim: …we just needed 50 or 100 feet more hose and we could have gotten around the back of the house. With the wind at our back we may have been able to save that house.

Art: After we left Meditation Mount we went to the Ojai Retreat. We had breakfast there and then decided to leave. The fire had come to us at the Mount, so it could come to the Ojai Retreat too, and we also wanted to leave before the mass exodus happened. There was just one road open out of town by the time we left, Highway 150. We went to Pismo Beach. Tim went to Santa Barbara and then to his brother's in Ventura.

Corinna: They were soaked and shivering cold when they got to the

Ojai Retreat on Tuesday morning. And Art didn't have a change of clothes. When we packed to leave he didn't pack anything to change into, and so he and Tim showed up wet from fighting the fire and from the backspray when the wind was so strong at their face. When we left we knew we would have to stop along the way to buy Art new clothes. We were in a caravan with another staff member who also had a pet bird so we just decided to keep driving north until we couldn't smell smoke anymore.

Art: When the fire burned through we were gone for a couple of days and then we came back and there was still fire going on. Two firefighters came up and they were scouting for hot spots. And there were signs of water spray on the auditorium and so we knew that there were resources here after we had left.

Corinna: In the end, we lost one duplex, about 70% of our gardens, damage to some of our iconic structures including our auditorium, and 28 acres of trees and webs of life on our wildlands. It was both harrowing and miraculous, because most of our buildings and the small areas of life around them didn't burn. If you looked down from the hill above the main grounds at the time, you would see an island of green in a sea of gray, with hillsides around looking like moonscapes with white ashy craters where trees used to

Photograph by Art Durand
The International Garden of Peace

be. But fires bring renewal, and this spring has been very graciously cool and more rainy than usual, which meant an abundant blossoming of green all around.

And, what couldn't burn was the sense of belonging to a larger whole. One sign of that was the way that our team members rallied both during and after the fire. It was truly inspiring. Even Tyler and Ali Sun, the couple who lost everything, never missed a beat in their service to the Mount after the fire. Another sign of that was the way our community came together to help each other. We met firefighters from all over the country who remarked about that. It makes us remember what a special place Ojai is, and how even in the face of trauma, belonging and caring can spring up and expand our willingness to give to one another.

Tim: There are always going to be natural disasters; it's just part of our existence. It is how you look at them and what you learn from them that is important. I felt like Art and I worked really well together as a team. We didn't have to talk much, we just both understood what had to be done and we did it.

Since Meditation Mount was founded in 1971, so many people who have come here have given their best and have learned so much and received so much, and it's all been with the best intentions. And that human energy, that conscious life force, it has given this place this heightened energy level. So many people who come here feel how special it is. It's not just the beautiful gardens; there are beautiful gardens everywhere. It's that spiritual dimension that exists up here. It's not complicated.

If we look at the plant kingdom we see that there is subtle communication between the plants and trees. And we look at the mineral kingdom and we see the connection between the rocks and the boulders. And we look at the animal kingdom and we see that they feel safe here. And we feel safe here. And because we consciously think in this way, and we work here in this way, we continue to create this intention and so this place holds this conscious commitment.

When I first came back up to the Mount, after the fire, I kept muttering, *it's a miracle, it's a miracle*. The fire came right up to the building, right up to the gardens and it stopped. One plant burned and nothing around it burned. There was a protection around the Mount. In morning meditation we speak about the Deva of the Mount, the Angel of the Mount, the spiritual protector of this place. And we play a part in this powerful connection. Because it is a result of our conscious awareness. We take care of this land and the natural phenomenon of that is that the land is aware of our participation.

I have the honor of being here, of living here and working here and so I am part of the process. As is everyone who comes here. Meditation Mount attracts people from all over the world. And we are not free from conflict, from human disagreements, but we come here and this place offers us the opportunity to ask, *what is the most loving thing that I can do? What is the most loving way that I can respond?*

Photograph by Art Durand
The Point— 'Joy is a Special Wisdom'

Artwork by Christopher King

AS DAYS GO BY

I am riding the waves of grief and overwhelming sorrow I feel for my Beloved Ojai—this special vortex oasis of majesty and healing—for the many who have literally lost everything but the shirts on their backs and for all the wildlife that has been lost, for the fear they must have felt on the ground as they ran from their homes, engulfed beneath their feet.

I mourn for the fox and deer and bobcat who walked so close to my windows, and perched upon boulders allowing me to behold their beauty and receive their medicine. For the bear I named Tonka who came right to my door several times. Days before the fire I saw him sniffing at my window, 3:00 am, lit by the full moon. For the pond where I meditated daily and experienced so much laughter from the comedy of ducks, now a thick black swamp of soot.

When I finally returned to Ojai, I was stricken first by the smell, but then by the black, barren land. A moonscape. My heart ached for Mother Nature. But mostly, I mourn for the trees, 'the Standing People,' as the Native Americans refer to them. They remind me daily to stand tall amidst the storm, to bend and sway when the proverbial winds blow, and to let go with grace like their leaves in Autumn. Fallen. Broken. Now ash.

Artwork and writing by Rene' Norman

Clockwise from top left: photographs by Emily Vedder, Norman Clayton and Nadia Natali

A tiny part of the interior of the stone library… eerily powdered and flaked.

Photograph and writing by Kate Mack

ASH

There is sadness in the air. It sits like smoke, unable to leave this quiet valley because no strong winds blow through our town. It is good, this lack of winds. Without strong winds there is less fire. But without strong winds there is this smoke. And this sadness.

It dances around the possibility and opportunity we see in front of us. We feel it here. Nestled in against ourselves and our town. We feel it and so we cover it with words of affirmation and support for each other and ourselves. We look to the future and plan how we will rebuild and notice how we connect and figure out what we can take from this ash and smoke to make a better place than the one we had before. But still there is this sadness.

It settles in our eyes and rides along our breath. I hear it in the rhythm of my step along the pavement as I walk in town. I see it in the eyes of the people around me. Both those that lost a great deal and those that lost just a bit in this—it is all relative to where we were and where we are going—and there is no quantitative way to measure that pain and the grief and really how do we comprehend what happened in this valley?

And so we sit in it. And so I sit in it. The sadness. And the discomfort of it. I cry, and I do not know half the time why the tears are there. And I go on social media even though I am overwhelmed by social media. And I give $50 to GoFundMe pages and YouCaring pages for people that I know and people that I do not know, too.

And I walk my dog and worry that the smoke I am keeping from my lungs with a mask of white with yellow bands does not fit her face, so she is breathing in this air of smoke. And breathing in this sadness, too. Falling from the sky like ash.

≈ Elizabeth Rose

Artwork by Soni Wright

A TIE-RAIL FOR HORSES
Amy Schneider

My beautiful 30-year-old daughter, Sara, died on March 2, 2017. Because she had a passion for horses her whole life (her second word after *mama* was *horse*), a tie-rail for horses with a memorial plaque was erected in her memory on the Wills Trail in the Ojai Valley Land Conservancy's Ventura River Preserve. It was completed two days before Thanksgiving, 12 days before

the fire started. Sara's dog Walter, who I now call 'our' dog, and I hiked out to see it on Thanksgiving morning. It was a hot day with near record breaking temperatures. The sun was shining through the oak trees, reflecting off of the copper plaque. Peaceful. Quiet. The wind whistling. Green leaves. Standing there in that moment, seeing Sara's memorial for the first time, I knew there was something very special about that spot.

Twelve days later, Monday, December 4th, I was sitting on the couch in the evening with Walter by my side. The phone began its bing-bing-binging with emergency alert notifications. Then the texts from friends and neighbors joined in the fray. And I just stayed sitting on my sofa. The power went out and still I sat. A few hours later I received my mandatory evacuation orders.

The last time I evacuated, in 2009, I gathered all of my important documents and I packed my car full with everything I could fit that had sentimental or monetary value. So I knew what I should do, but I felt different this time. I continued to sit. Calmly. On the couch. I wasn't really thinking clearly about the possibility of losing my home and everything in it, because in the big scheme of life, losing 'things' as opposed to life, my daughter's life, seemed so unimportant to me. This time, besides my computer, I only took two things with me: my favorite framed photograph of Sara and our dog, Walter.

I got up and walked out to my car with the photograph tucked under one arm and Walter in the other. Driving down our road, I thought about my neighbor who I was sure was asleep. I turned around and went back to get her. Unable to get her attention with the doorbell or my pounding on the door, I went looking around for the search and rescue team who I knew were going door to door. When I found them, they came over and were able to rouse her. She came to the door a little bit disoriented but she agreed to leave with me and go to my friends' house on the other side of the Valley.

In the morning she realized she had left home without some necessities so we headed back to Tower Drive. By the time we got to our neighborhood our road was already closed but we were let in with our promise that we would get what we needed and get out quickly. As we drove up our road we could see the fire right behind our homes. We followed instructions. We got in and we got out.

My neighbor did not want to leave the area. So I parked my car on Carne Road where we had a perfect view of our homes and the fire coming ever so much closer. She was very upset and asked me why I was so calm. *That's just me, I'm calm in a crisis.* She said *but look at the fire, our houses are going to burn down.* I told her our homes were not going to burn down. And then, because I told her that, I had to do something.

I got out of my car and stood in the middle of Ojai Avenue. When the next fire truck came I didn't move. Basically the driver had to stop unless he wanted to run me over. So he stopped. I went to his window, pointed to our homes and asked if he could please go up there and save them. He said they were on their way to Upper Ojai and he would call it in. So he drove off. I stayed in the middle of the road and repeated my actions when the next truck drove up. The person driving this truck told me they didn't have water and that I should look for a yellow fire truck. So I continued standing in the middle of the road. The next truck was the right color. I stopped them. I pointed, repeating my appeal. I stepped away and watched them take a right turn up

Photograph by Tania Parker
Ventura River Preserve

Tower Drive. And soon after that, several trucks followed. We ended up with a team in each of our driveways. They saved our homes. The fire came six feet away from the back door of one neighbor's home and down the driveway of another. It was very, very close. The firefighters worked hard and saved our neighborhood. We were some of the fortunate ones.

I was evacuated for five days and when I came home the air in my home and in the Valley was intolerable. At the same time my mother became ill and was admitted to a hospital in Florida. So I decided to leave home and go help take care of her while keeping up with all of the fire news from far away. I knew that almost all of the Ventura River Preserve had burned and I wondered about Sara's memorial tie-rail and the peaceful sweet spot in which it sat. I didn't want to bother anyone at the Land Conservancy to ask because I knew how busy they all must have been. So, really I just thought about it and hoped for the best.

An unexpected email landed in my inbox on December 22nd with the subject 'The Plaque Survived!' I opened the email from Tania at the Land Conservancy and was so amazed to see photos of Sara's spot. The tie-rail and plaque, a nearby bench and the canopy of the oaks above the tie-rail all survived the fire. This sweet little dell in the middle of acres of devastation somehow survived. This time I did cry. I don't hold any specific thoughts about life after death, but I do feel open to the possibilities of the unknown. And all I know is that it really felt like Sara was working her magic from somewhere out there. It was such a beautiful gift in the midst of so much loss.

The notion of the loss of things as opposed to that of a life… it's thoroughly heartbreaking no matter what kind of loss it is. The grieving process affects us all at some point in our lives and for so many different reasons. A life lived will always include both joy and sorrow. It would have hurt me terribly if I'd lost my home. But I didn't. And I'm so grateful, because even though I sat on that couch thinking I'd already lost the most important thing in my life, and nothing else mattered, the truth is that I still get to read Sara's poetry and see her paintings on my walls. I get to look at photographs of her. They make me laugh and they make me cry.

So many homes with so many treasured memories are forever gone because of the Thomas Fire. One family that I know lost everything. And I happened to have pictures of their daughter when she was a young girl. She was Sara's friend. I put those photos in an envelope and put them in their mailbox. Just a tiny gesture. To have a memory to actually hold onto is precious.

Sara's memorial, surviving in the midst of so much destruction, reminds me that joy is always interwoven with grief and that grief can bring us to a place in which our hearts are truly opened more deeply than ever before.

Photograph by Tania Parker
Ventura River Preserve

SMOKY SUNSET

I returned to Ojai the day the Thomas Fire began. Driving home I saw large bright orange flames with big black billows of smoke as early as the Conejo Grade. The drive home was hauntingly beautiful and as the days unfolded I knew that it was a rare opportunity to capture amazing photographs, but it was so horrible and I just could not photograph it.

There were many days we would leave and come back, and we would survey what was happening and then leave again. I did take some ashy photographs during this time and also some of the smoke in the distance. I do not feel any regret that I was unable to photograph the fire but I am so grateful that other people captured the fire in this way.

Photograph and writing by Deborah Lyon

IT IS NOT ABOUT THE LOSS OF THINGS

It's 3:00 am and I can't sleep. I have to force myself to eat. It is not just the loss of things—hard goods in a room where you walked and sat. It's alone at 2:00 am in a refuge house with other people's comforts and you have a sudden stab, knowing you can't rest on the pillow that so perfectly cradles your sleeping head.

It's the chain smoking after 20 years of self-righteous abstinence and the surrendering to self-pity when all you want is to be grateful for your life. It's not the things really.

It's the ground and trees who have carried your burden, become the bridge to your soul, now blackened and charred like an ashy fireplace that just days ago gave warmth. It's sitting on curbs on the side of the road, because the people you see shopping will cook dinner in their homes. It's grief stumbling down a path you've never seen. It's the friend who gives a hug and then goes about her day.

I wish I'd had a family. I wish there was a lover in my bed. I want to be held.

It's not about the cookware or the rug or the rings you'll never wear. It's the vision of the future and the pieces of your past. The letters three decades old, folded in that special box with a strand of your dead brother's hair. It's the book you read three times, and the book you will no longer write.

Be grateful. All things pass. Life is never certain, nothing ever lasts. Yet we survive by a denial—a deal forced on us at birth—to be mirrored makes us real, without it we are lost.

From year to year, we lay the flagstones, captured moments hold us on the ground. Grow wings? Freedom from attachments? The persimmon tree I sat beneath is gone. There were the photo albums confirming I was loved. And the window I looked out of, seeing grace in flowers who endure their death and yet return.

≽ *Kiera Van Gelder*

Photograph by Norman Clayton

Photograph by Dave May
Chief Peak

Photograph by Esther van der Werf
Topa Topa

Dana inherited this Madonna from his Godmother. It is a small miracle that it somehow remained on the windowsill surrounded by melted glass and twisted metal. It is a message of strength, faith and grace.

Photograph and writing by Dawn Ceniceros

Even in the resilience of mountains
there lies vulnerability.
Charred, empty, broken;
pockets ridden by ash,
hidden by a smoke-filled sky.

⇒ *Lori Hansen*

Photographs by Judy Gabriel

METAPHORS FOR THE CHANGING

Today I was able to visit my home and begin the process of letting go, yet there were unexpected gifts when I arrived. Yes, all the buildings had been destroyed, but the land felt open and cleansed. As I explored each area with an eye to my camera, I found the emotional upset I anticipated transformed into creative observing and art. There were colors, textures, reveals, juxtapositions, skeletal remains and beauty everywhere I looked. Are all my belongings ash? Yes. Are there bits and pieces strewn about in a hodgepodge of twisted melted forms? Yes. Are there objects unmarred and napping in the aftermath of the fiery onslaught? Absolutely. And… there is curiosity and wonder.

It's a challenging time, simultaneous feelings of displacement and complete liberation. Untethered to the things that may have defined me, yet missing the sanctity of my mountain home and spacious land. There's something available here, entering into the sacred heart of the fire, possibilities that have yet to reveal themselves.

Remaining in the adventure of newness and awareness that there are many unknown opportunities before me is challenging at times. The creative thoughts and ideas that generally come easily have been taking a bit more than usual to summon. Yet, things aren't usual, there is no normal. It's a reminder to relax and embrace the simple things that present themselves every day, simple things to be grateful for. Perspective, always.

Maybe that's what this really is all about. This home, these hills, metaphors for the changing, the shiftings, the burning away of what no longer serves me/us, individually or communally.

Photograph and writing by Ray Powers

The fire transformed my 1950's cornet into a beautiful patina, a visual art rather than a sonic one.
It's a different kind of blue, an improv born from the blazing lips of Thomas.

Photograph and writing by Ray Powers

During the fire, there were red, orange, clouds of colored smoke.
Neon sunsets. All color.

After the fire I found variations of blackness. Ash grey, charcoal, pitch, soot, slate, jet.

The ultimate darkest color opens the door to mystery and prepares you for the unknown.
It radiates power.
Elegance.

Artwork and writing by Sherry Loehr
Photograph by James Bryan Davis

She fixed her gaze upon me and decided to curl up and rest and stayed about twenty minutes. She came from the high country with that long winter coat, but was obviously burned in spots. It was so sad. I have agonized about the loss of animals here in the Canyon. I have been here sixteen years and they are all my friends. I am still grieving about it... the animals were surrounded by fire with no place to go.

Left to right: photograph and writing by Victoria Aja, photograph by Stephanie Reynolds

PERHAPS I AM AN INGRATE

I do not want to
chant OM
or visualize my
root chakra

while a man
at the front
with a drum

creates a sacred
container he ensures
us is safe

as we're guarded by
his 12 personal
archangels.

I do not want to
be told how I
should feel, by

names on a screen
as I scroll through
options and resource sites

Photograph by Kiera Van Gelder

while I look for the
voices of our soul.

I do not want to
stand in grocery lines
listening to shoppers

listing the things
they put in their cars,
while sighing with relief

that all, thank god, is well.
I do not want to be told
that the sea of ashes
which used to be my words

are the soil of land's regrowth.
I know that well enough.

I want a circle of raw suffering—
to speak and listen from the heart.

I want a coven of witnesses
spinning webs of love
from all this grief.

≈ *Kiera Van Gelder*

Photograph by Kiera Van Gelder

Ours was the only property on that hill that burned, the sacrificial lamb, burning to save others. My late husband and I have owned this land since 2003. In all those years we were never able to hike to the top because the chaparral was so thick. After the fire, the entire one-acre lot looked like a moonscape. Bare and black, but beautiful in its rawness. We could see these amazing boulders for the first time, along with the spectacular view of the Valley and beyond.

We built this house (right) with our own hands. My husband was an engineer; he designed it. I remember pouring that retaining wall and everything else about that project. It was the last project we did together before he died. Although I do not know the family who was living there my heart aches for their loss, and for my own.

Photographs and writing by Karen McMahon
Top and lower left: Top of Foothill Road. Lower right: North Fork Springs Road.

Photograph by Pamela Luna

Photograph by Robin Catherine Lawson
Opposite page: photograph by Kathleen Collins

Our Community Comes Together

FLUX: SACRED DISQUIET

My children and I survived the La Conchita landslide in 2005 that claimed ten of my neighbors including Michelle Wallet, found surrounded by her three young daughters. The loss of security and life from the Thomas Fire and mudslides in Montecito brought it all back. I feel this community's journey in a palpable crushing sensation but also as a joyfully transcendent reworking, bonding and rebirth. Like our small town surrounded by forest, I see us as a common mind living in a lush wilderness of emotional experience, both beautiful and terrifying in its powerfully changing harmonies. Here is to our passionate engagement with each other and nature. We are transformed by weather patterns, most deeply and lastingly from those within. Art is my controlled burn, soul connection and flowering. Ojai's resilient loving embrace is true home.

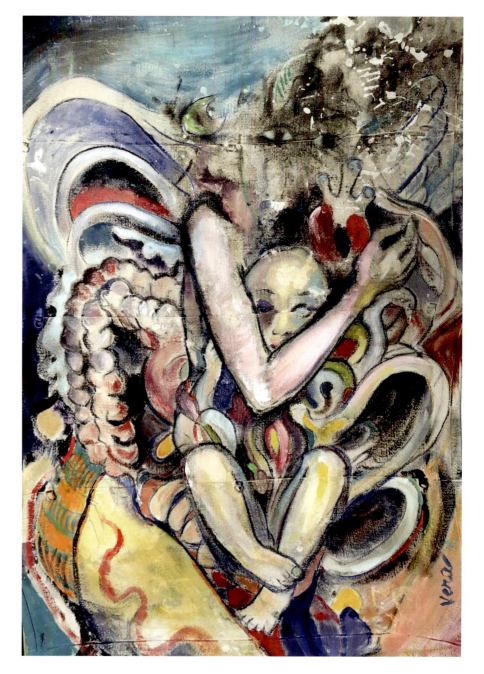

Artwork and writing by Vera Long

Gareth Williams
Fly-Hope-Dream
May 11, 2018

I founded Fly-Hope-Dream as a way to give back to families who have lost a child. Whether to illness, accident, suicide or murder, that loss is so great. I understand this because I lost my youngest son, Timmy, in 2008. I wanted to give to others in a way that would allow them to feel joy and a sense of peace, and to gain perspective by being up in the air.

My organization is based at Santa Paula Airport and that is where I was when I got a call from Billy, my good friend and landlord, that he'd heard reports of a fire and was going to check them out. I waited about half an hour and then called him again but got a dead signal, so I called another friend who was renting a room from me. He was home at the property, but did not know about the fire yet. After we checked online he said he was going to leave.

Another half hour went by and I was getting concerned. More information was appearing online that the fire was near Thomas Aquinas College and I realized that I could no longer get to my house by going up Route 150 through Santa Paula. I opted for the long route via Ojai and headed off down Route 126 towards Ventura. I could see the flames in the mountains above Santa Paula. When I had made it as far as Route 33 and into Casitas Springs, I got a call from Billy's wife that she had been evacuated and had rescued my dogs. We met at Vons in Ojai and then I drove back the way I came, with the dogs, to the airport. When I got to Wells Road the fire was already there. It had taken the flames only 40 minutes to move all that way.

I stayed that night at my office in the airport and early the next morning, at around 7:00 am, I got a call from Billy telling me that everything was gone. That is when I learned that I lost everything. It was difficult to comprehend. I literally had lost everything I owned. I had three saxophones and a clarinet, all gone. I lost all our family videos. All my clothes, except the shorts and polo shirt I was wearing. I had nothing. I had to go out and buy everything. It was just me and my dogs.

About two or three weeks after the fire, I was having a conversation with another person who had lost their home and she was saying how someone had said to her, when she commented about losing all her family photos, *well, at least you still have your memories*. And that was a trigger for me, because that is what you often hear when you lose a child. People try to be supportive but no one can truly understand unless they have been through child loss themselves. I realized in that moment, hearing that comment, that surviving a wildfire is a similar experience. As with child loss, the only ones who can truly empathize are fellow survivors. And other people, while they are always well-meaning, don't know what to say.

I decided to expand the Fly-Hope-Dream mission to include those who lost their homes in the Thomas Fire. I know from experience that if you get people up in the air, the experience will blow them away. Being 1,000 feet above the ground gives a person a whole new perspective. Literally and figuratively. I want to share that with fire survivors and give them the opportunity to see what has happened to them from a different viewpoint. From in the air.

We can't control what happens to us but we can decide how we are going to respond. And often we need to see things from a new vantage point before we can respond in a new way. Flying gives people that opportunity.

The worst thing about this process—I'll talk about losing a child first—the first week between the death and the funeral, everyone is all over you and then for a week or two afterwards everyone is looking after you. But then suddenly everything is back to normal and everyone has gone back to their lives and you're left with this *new normal*. A normal that you never wanted and wouldn't wish on your worst enemy. And I'm seeing the same thing happening with the fire. How many people even remember the Thomas Fire now? Most have moved on. But those who have lost so much, they are still struggling almost every day.

Photograph by Domonic Dean Breaux

Zhena Muzyka
June 27, 2018

I had decided to surprise my husband for his 50th birthday with a trip to New York. I had a meeting with my publishing house and so combined the two trips. He didn't know where we were going until we checked in at the airport. I was so excited to treat him; I had booked all these great shows and we were going to go to museums—all those things that New York is great for. We got in late Monday night and I woke up on Tuesday morning (5:00 am East Coast time) to all these texts from my son, who was in Ojai with my daughter and my mom on Foothill. *Mom, there's a fire in Santa Paula.* And then the next one, *Hey Mom, I can see the sky glowing but it's all the way in Santa Paula so that doesn't make sense.* And then, *Mom, I can actually see flames.* And finally, *Mom, I haven't heard from you, so I guess I'm going to go to bed.* I'm looking at this and I'm thinking *oh my god* and I call my mom and I call my son and no one is answering the phone because they're sleeping now—it's 2:00 in the morning in Ojai. I look online and I can see the terror and how fast this fire is moving. All I can think of is my kids.

I finally got hold of my mom and told her to get the kids and get the pets and get out. *Oh dear god*, she said, *there's fire everywhere.* My dad was a Forest Service firefighter. My mom knows fire. She gets my kids and the dogs in the car and they go to Lompoc, where we are originally from.

It's now 9:00 am in New York and I have this meeting to go to. I flew to New York to present a book from an author that lives here in Ojai. Right before the meeting starts I text the author about the book presentation and she texts back, *my house is gone, the farm is gone, the animals are gone.* She had rescue animals—horses and pigs and burros. I didn't know what to do. Do I present? Do I leave? What? While I am sitting in this state of shock she proceeds to elegantly answer my question in three beautifully written text paragraphs.

My author kept her cool to write such a beautiful response to my inquiry, the least I could do was keep mine and successfully present her book to our team. It was probably one of the best presentations of my life. For her. Then I showed my boss what was happening in Ojai and then I started figuring out how to get home.

I didn't know if my home was going to make it. My husband was going to ask a friend to go to the house and grab things for us but there was nothing that I wanted. My kids and my animals were safe. And I realized that this and the safety of my town and my people—the people here in Ojai—that this was all that was important.

That night my neighbor called and said the fire was desperately close to our homes. I sent out an emergency text to my women's circle: *please bring all your goddess power, energy and visualization power and envision a circle of cold blue air encircling Ojai.* After exhaustion overtook me, I finally crashed. Two hours later, I woke up and my friend's husband had sent us a video text where he was standing next to our home with the fire chief showing us that it was okay. My husband and I cried tears of relief, but to me at this point the house was less important than I'd realized. When asked what I wanted, there was nothing I could think of other than my kids and my pets. The fire clarified my values.

Thursday morning at JFK, I told the TSA woman that our house had just been saved by firefighters, and she said, *now you have to praise God in thanks every day.* I definitely agree. We got home Thursday. That afternoon the fire came from the other direction. We live on the Pratt Trail and so the fire was right there. Our neighbor's vineyards actually ended up saving our property, but there were flames and smoldering for a long time. We would go out and stomp them down for days.

Friday night, friends and I arranged a meeting at Azu. We put up these huge poster boards and on one we wrote WHAT I HAVE TO OFFER and on the other we wrote WHAT I NEED and we set up stations all around the restaurant. So many people showed up. More people wrote offers than needs, and we were able to raise tens of thousands of dollars that night alone for HELP of Ojai. I loved seeing this. It gave me hope in humanity. It showed me that our spirit is stronger than our divisiveness. I have been here for 21 years and I have loved Ojai from day one and getting to see the quality of the people in this town under this kind of pressure was beautiful.

Photograph by Brian Aikens for the Ojai Valley Museum

Angela Hanline and Franki D. Williams with Greg Cooper
Humane Society of Ventura County, Ojai
April 18 and May 2, 2018

Angela: I left work on Monday of the fire and went down to Ventura. When I came back up the 33, I saw the smoke. I called our director and I said, *I'll meet you at the shelter, there's a fire* and so I was already here waiting when everybody showed up. We knew it was going to be a long night, but we had no idea it was going to be so massive.

Franki: I received a phone call from our directors. It was about 8:00 pm. They said that a fire had broken out in Upper Ojai. I went right to the shelter and by the time I got there most of the staff was already there. And animals had already started coming in.

Angela: Within a couple of hours, we realized how bad it really was. I instantly put posts on Facebook saying that we are open and please bring your animals here to safety. We just got the word out right away. We had horses coming in literally within 20 minutes of putting the posts up on Facebook. That first night I think we got at least 50 horses. We were zip-tying corrals together—as fast as these horses would come in we would just tie them in. It was pretty insane.

Franki: That first night we lost our electricity and the fire alarm was going the whole time. We put a call out through our staff for volunteers to come and help. I honestly don't know who a lot of the volunteers were, so many people came. They came with trucks and trailers and they helped set up corrals as the majority of the animals coming in were large animals.

Angela: We had goats, sheep, llamas and alpacas coming in.

Franki: We got close to 30 goats—that was interesting, trying to herd them all into a pen. In the dark. Our electricity was still out, but we did it. And while most people were able to take their dogs and cats with them, we did receive those pets too.

And then a lot of the work was feeding, mucking stalls, caring for the livestock—the horses and alpacas. At first getting so many animals out into those corrals was difficult. We ended up just doubling up and doubling up, and tying the corralling together to make more pens for the horses. The entire hill behind us was burning but these animals did great.

After that first night, a lot of the additional dogs and cats that came were here because their owners had lost their homes. Or they could not go back to their homes and so they brought in their pets and slept in their cars or in trailers in our parking lot. They had their animals here but they didn't want to just drop them off and so they stayed and helped care for their own animals and helped us as well.

Angela: My daughter went out with Steven, he drives a trailer for us, and they were driving through the fire to get the horses out off of Rice Road and off of Creek Road. In some places there was fire on both sides of the road and they were driving to get those horses out to safety. A lot of people own animals, but they don't have transportation for them. During the fire we provided all of that for them.

Franki: In total we went from 80 animals to close to 400 animals. So over 300 evacuees. We have 48 dog kennels and most of them were already filled before the fire and so we had to double up, with some of the dogs inside and some of the dogs kept outside in the caged area attached to each inside dwelling. And then we had all of the play yards filled with horses and goats and pigs and alpacas and so the dogs were unable to play. Which was okay because we had so many animals that we did not know a lot about—who was vaccinated, who was spayed and neutered... We couldn't just bring them all together anyway.

Photograph by Franki D. Williams
Humane Society of Ventura County, Ojai

Angela: Tuesday night was hard because the fire came over the hill on our side of the Valley, but it was Wednesday night that was the most difficult for me. I lost my parents within the last two years, within ten months of each other. I lost my mom and three months later I lost my stepdad and then ten months after my mom died, my dad died. I climbed up on the roof, the whole mountain was on fire, and I said, out loud, *I'm not ready so you better do something*. And the fire came down but then it stopped. And it completely bypassed us. It was amazing.

I just prayed to whoever was listening. I said, *you know what, it's not our time, we've got these animals and you have to go away*. Because we would not have evacuated. We would have stayed here with the animals and fought the fire. The firefighters would have been here if we needed them. And we have a tank. We would have dealt with it. With the horses, if we had let them go, they would run away from the fire, but all the other animals, they needed us. None of us were going anywhere. We were just going to be right here.

Franki: We really relied on our volunteers and our community, and they came from all over the state. We had volunteers from San Diego and from Sacramento. They would come and walk the dogs so at least they had some exercise. Some volunteers would sit in the kennels and just be with the dogs. And with all these volunteers, we ended up having another problem—how are we going to house all these people and how are we going to feed all these people that are here doing all this work? So we put another call out. And we had so many in the community help.

Angela: We received incredible financial support. We received blankets and towels, toothbrushes and shampoo. People were bringing in food supplies and the community stepped in and were feeding us. We had Café Emporium bring us breakfasts and lunches. And Ojai Beverage Company brought us sandwiches.

Franki: We had caterers from Los Angeles that were coming and bringing vegan buffets, and people in the community were donating food items and canned goods. Our entire patio was filled.

And then it got out that we were a hub in Ojai, not just for animals but for anybody who wanted to help but didn't know what to do. All these people ended up here and we did our best to work them into our organization, give them jobs to do and include them in the support that was coming from others here. They did not just donate their time, they donated supplies. We were getting clothes and diapers and so many other things. We had become a drop-off center. It was great, and we were able to make it work but it was a lot of work. After a while we started communicating with HELP of Ojai and Upper Ojai Relief and taking a lot of the goods that we were getting and dispersing them into the community through these other relief centers.

Angela: There were four of us that were here the entire time. I was here for ten days. I never went home. And then I ended up getting injured. But I still came in every day. I just wasn't allowed to work with the animals. I was able to do computers and answer phones and things like that.

Franki: Two things went through our minds during the fire: there's certainly your own personal fear—there is fire and it's scary and your family and friends are evacuating—and then there is the who we are and what our job is in the community. And these are two different things. We are very confident in our abilities; we have trained for this. We have the supplies that we need for this. We have our shelter director, Jolene Hoffman, who has been here 30-plus years and has gone through this before and so even though there is that part of you that is worried and scared, as an organization we were always confident.

Frankie: Our work continued for weeks into 2018. For the people who lost their homes, their animals were here for a very long time. And we also took evacuees in from Santa Barbara as the fire continued to move north.

We had a couple of interesting animal cases. We had a stray horse. His owners never came forward. He was found wandering alone in Santa Paula when the fire hit down there. We nursed him back to health and he was just adopted. And then we had Mike. He was brought in on the second night of the fire, carried in to our front counter; this poor dog had burns on all four paws.

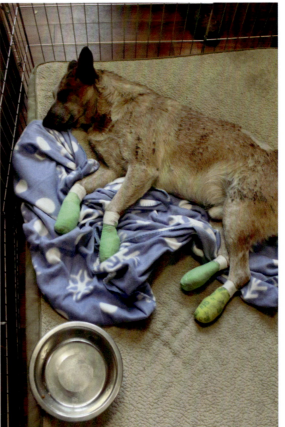

Photograph by Franki D. Williams
Humane Society of Ventura County, Ojai

Photograph by Franki D. Williams
Humane Society of Ventura County, Ojai

He had already been seen by a vet, Dr. Karen Moore, DVM, and his paws were already wrapped. I believe that the barn on the property that he was on had burned and he was likely hiding under the barn because he was covered in roofing tar. The vet who took care of him initially, and wrapped his paws, could not keep him and so he was brought to us. And we took him in under our care and had a vet tech, Jenna Wedemeyer, assigned to him 24/7 who cared for him and slept with him on the office floor and he became a special animal for us. We had a vet from Santa Barbara, Dr. Heather Rally, coming in to volunteer with us and she checked him out and made some calls and figured out financial support for him and took over his care and she eventually adopted him.

Angela: This past Friday the last of the animals went home. These were the people who lost absolutely everything and were only just now able to take their animals. So now, after five months, things are getting back to normal.

Franki: The sense of community was overwhelming. The fact that we could do this work, that we were pulling this off, I was so proud of every single one of us. A lot of our staff and our volunteers had been evacuated. We had staff members who couldn't go home, they were here 24 hours a day. We were sleeping on dog beds in the office and everyone stayed in good spirits. We were all there for each other. When it was over I almost missed that comradeship—our staff, our volunteers, so many new people. I am so proud of all of our staff and our volunteers. Everyone just pulled together and, though it could be tense and everyone was tired, we all worked together. We were committed to these animals and we weren't going anywhere.

We never were in the mandatory evacuation zone. We were very close, but we were never told we had to leave. We are also surrounded by a golf course and storage units so as far as the fire creeping in to us, we were pretty well protected. And never at any point would we endanger anybody in the community. We were in very close contact with the sheriff's department and the fire department, keeping aware of what was happening, and so we certainly were aware of any kind of issues that threatened our facility.

Angela: For me it was an honor to be here at the Humane Society and care for all these animals. People are bringing their pets here, they believe in us enough that they will bring us their animals. Their animals are their family. I wouldn't want somebody to walk away from my family and I am not going to walk away from theirs. I would never do it. Any disaster, it doesn't matter, that's why we're here, that's why we do what we do.

Photograph by Franki D. Williams
Humane Society of Ventura County, Ojai

Reno Rolle
BoKU
April 9, 2018

When I first learned that the fire broke out in Santa Paula, we were focused on helping neighbors, moving horses, goats, cutting brush from the side of people's houses. And I posted on the community page that we had room: We have two acres, so if someone needs to park their car, their trailer, they can certainly feel free to utilize our lot for that, and for animals, too. We have a big gated area, bring your animals here, they can be safe here. I also wanted the community to know that we have young, strong guys. Between my son and my son-in-law and friends and employees, these guys are all young and strong and wonderful and are always there to help.

So, we're running around, trying to figure out what the fire is doing and figure out what our plan is, and we had a friend drop in, a neighbor, and she walked into our house and was like, *oh my god, the air is so good in here*. And I looked, and we had this Air Doctor air purifier in our living room. It had been in here for about a year and I never paid a lot of attention to it. I essentially had taken it for granted until this neighbor of mine said, *oh my god, the air in your house is so wonderful*.

The filter light had changed to yellow when usually it's blue, and the fan was running higher. This thing was really working. And my friend asked me, *where did you get this thing?*

My friend Peter Spiegel had invented this years ago, and I immediately called him up and asked him how many he had. There were eight in his office. I sent an employee down to grab those eight and the minute they showed up in my driveway they were gone.

I called him again and asked him, *how many of these can we get quickly? There was a real problem here in Ojai with the air quality*. He said his warehouse down in Chino had 1,500–2,000. I told him to send me a truckload.

So he arranges for this truck to come up the next day for $200–300. I post again on the community page that we have access to these air purifiers, that we will share them at our cost, and that they were arriving at BoKU tomorrow afternoon by 2:00 pm. Then I get a phone call, the truck service raised their price to $600. They complained about traffic and the fire.

And when I explained that our town is on fire and we're trying to share these air purifiers because people need them, and that the man who makes them is selling them to us at a very discounted price and we're selling them at our cost, none of this landed. I hung up the phone and called my son and had him pull the seats out of the bus and drive down to Chino, three and a half hours each away.

I posted again on the community page about the delay and when the air purifiers would get here, and by the time my son got back people were standing in line waiting for these things to arrive. That's when it started. There are some incredible people in the world, and many of them live right here in Ojai. And this became very obvious. We are blessed to live where we are.

One woman came in and said that she wanted to buy three air purifiers. And I said, *okay, fine*, and explained the machine, told her we could load them in her car. And she said, *no, they're not for me*. And, still not understanding, I said, *okay, can we arrange delivery or help you in some way?* And she said, *well, I don't know who they are for yet, but someone will come in that needs them and I want to buy them now, so they are here for these people*. It was incredible. And that happened more than once.

This woman paid for three that we were able to share to those in need, and she sort of set this beautiful thing in motion with the process really focusing on charity and goodwill and what we were really doing and what the core meaning behind the whole process was. And we began doing the same thing, reaching out to people who didn't have the means but still had the need. Because we were in a position to help them.

What started as one truck load, turned into close to 1,500 of these units to homes and families in Ojai. From our perspective, as a family, it was an unbelievable experience to do something incredibly meaningful to help

Photograph by Norman Clayton

people. This experience is something I'll never personally forget. Our family, we will never forget.

To experience it the way that we did, with dust masks and loading the purifiers and delivering them to people who were clearly struggling, and you'd plug them on and it starts whirring away and immediately turns red. This is what that experience for us is all about—making a positive difference, being in a position to help.

Throughout the entire experience, we were overwhelmed with people thanking us and expressing their gratitude and it was a tricky place because we felt this, *no, thank you!* It was so hard to articulate or express how we felt because we were overwhelmed with gratitude that we were able to be in this position to help.

I am thanking God and thanking the universe because I realize that 25 years ago, when I met Peter Spiegel, this is why I met him. This is why. Because 25 years later, I would be living in this beautiful town that is on fire and he would have the answer. He would have the solution, and I would be in the position to do this for so many people. It was just priceless. I can't even begin to put a value on the opportunity to positively impact our community. It is so profound.

And now, I recall it and I get that wonderful warm feeling again. As terrible as it was and as frightening as it was and as stressful, it was probably the best two weeks, the best month, that I can recall because of what it did to connect us as a community. And because of what we saw in people; the goodwill in our community. People's desire to help, we saw it coming out everywhere. I mean the whole vibe changed. Ojai is a beautiful place, and in this tragedy the best came out in so many people.

One woman that came in put it best. She said, *when Mother Nature is at her worst, humanity is at its best.* I will never forget that; it captured the essence of what we were experiencing in the best way possible.

We take a lot of it for granted, but when you are living it and you see how the police and the firemen and the first responders—you see how they have dedicated their lives to saving and protecting us—when you experience that first hand, you go deeper in gratitude and begin to understand there are people out there who dedicate their lives to helping others and boy, it reminds you to do what you can when you can.

And this is worth commemorating. Because we'll move on and the fire will become part of history, but when we recall it, it is a reminder of what's really important. When we recall it, we will remember that being in this experience, it was a perspective and priority shift, as what you thought was so important, it changes. And things really start to realign.

Photograph by Jeffrey Stuteville

Photograph by Clay White

LIVING THROUGH THE FIERY BLAZE

This fire has taken much away from us, but it has also created a sense of community I've never experienced before. I have sat at tables with strangers who became instant friends. We bonded together through tragedy. People's hearts are open wide offering kindness to whomever they meet. The message of this powerful fire has affected everyone differently but we are all in this together. We have shared the tragedy of loss but gained friendship and community.

⇒ *Karina Aroha*

COMMUNITY

Standing there in the middle of town nearly alone, coughing and struggling to see in front of me, I was resolved that as long as our people were safe and away from this pending danger, our community would survive this tragedy. It is the people that make our city so great, it is not the bricks and mortar.

⇒ *Johnny Ortez-Tibbels*

Left to right: photographs by Johnny Ortez-Tibbels and Jeffrey Stuteville (Camp Ramah)

NEW MOON NECKLACE

Like most Ojai residents, the Love Heals team had to evacuate during the fires and our store remained closed during most of December. But on one of the days when the fires peaked, I drove back to Ojai from Santa Barbara. Love Heals was desolate and very smoky. No one was in town. It looked like a war and there was no mask that could shelter enough for my mild asthma. But I was on a mission.

Barely breathing, I designed a simple necklace that would evoke our Valley of the Moon and at the same time could be affordable to many. I ran to my photography studio on Bryant Street and managed to do some photography. By the next morning the New Moon Necklace campaign was on.

We posted to Facebook: Reaching out to those affected by the Thomas Fire in Ventura County. From now until Christmas, with every necklace sold, we will donate one to any family that has been affected by the Thomas Fire. We want everyone to have a holiday and are honored to share our New Moon necklace: imbued with lunar magic to evoke the healing essence of the Ojai Valley.

It was so touching and amazing to feel and witness the response we got. It was an absolute success. A week after, right before Christmas, we were able to donate 50 necklaces to the relief station in Upper Ojai. Eventually, when we opened the store, many more people came to get their necklaces. It warms my heart to see locals around town wearing our New Moon necklace. We were honored to be able to help our community through this time of so much loss and devastation.

Necklace and writing by Mariana Schulze

Photograph by Maeve Juarez

Kim Stroud
Ojai Raptor Center
May 9, 2018

This was not my first fire, we had been through three fires before, so we knew we had to get out. We packed our dogs and cats and we went over to the Raptor Center. This was early Tuesday morning; the fire was coming over the hill and down onto Creek Road near our home.

By Tuesday afternoon the smoke was bad and the prediction was that the fire was coming towards the Center. If it were just us, no animals, we might have waited but when you have animals, when you have other beings depending on you, you move. And so we loaded all the birds into the Center's van. It took two hours to load 24 birds. We had to release 16 birds back into the wild. This was hard for us. We like to release them back to where they came from as much as possible. We were waiting for rides, and then the fire came and we had to release any birds that could fly because we didn't have enough cages for all the patients that still needed our care. So we gathered up all the birds that could fly and sent them out into the Valley. The Raptor Center is located along the Ventura River where there is a corridor, so the birds could have gone south or towards Lake Casitas or north. We said *you better fly away*.

We loaded the remaining birds and then we heard that the fire had jumped Highway 101 near Faria Beach and we weren't sure where to go so we held position where we were. We never lost power and so we could hear the news and we decided to stay. This was now 7:00 pm Tuesday. We unloaded the birds from the van and back into the Center. We set them up in our hospital and reloaded when we decided to leave, which was what we had to do later that night.

We started to leave and then discovered that they had just shut Highway 33 at Encino Road. Because we couldn't get out on the 33 we tried Burnham Road thinking we'd go down Santa Ana Road but we had to turn around there too; the police had shut down Santa Ana at the Corner Market. The 150 was still open towards Carpinteria but we didn't know anyone there that could house all of us and the animals.

We went back to the Center and we unloaded again and hunkered down, taking shifts watching the fire and the smoke. And then at about 5:00 am Wednesday morning my daughter called me. She had been watching videos of the fire and she shared with me that Creek Road was toast.

There was so much media hype and misinformation. I heard that the Thacher School had completely burned down and Besant Hill School was burned down and Boccali's restaurant was gone. I wanted to find out if Creek Road was as bad as we were hearing, so I drove over and went around the police barrier to check our home. Our house was still there.

I grabbed the dog beds and went back to the Center and then on Wednesday night the fire started over the mountain on the other side of the Valley from Creek Road. The smoke was so bad and we decided to go to Ventura. We had a volunteer who offered for us to come to her home; she had created space in her dining room for all our birds. We were there for four days and then returned to the Center on Saturday.

We unloaded the birds but we couldn't put them outside because of their delicate respiratory systems so they all had to go into the hospital area. The eagle went onto a perch on the floor along with a few other birds and everyone else went into racks in the hospital.

My sister and I went home

Photograph by Tania Parker
Ojai Valley Land Conservancy

with the dogs and cats. We had no power but we had gas and candles. I went back to the Center and was told that we were at risk again. This was when the fire was heading towards Carpinteria and Santa Barbara. I was not going to spend another night watching the fire and loading and unloading the birds so I put them all back in the van and drove them over to our house.

On Sunday morning I took them back to the Center one last time. We had to run air purifiers but at least we were back where the birds were safe and we had everything we needed to take care of them.

We had very little help during the constant evacuations; it was amazing that things worked out. We had a master evacuation plan which we are now changing to create a better phone tree that includes volunteers that do not live in Ojai, because those that live here were having to take care of their own family and their own items. We need an evacuation plan that includes places where we can keep all of our birds together. With this fire we were getting offers to bring three birds one place, four birds another place... but that meant splitting our birds and we want to keep them together.

We were very lucky that the fire happened when it did because we did not have a lot of patients. In July we will have approximately 270 birds and babies. We would not have been able to move that many birds during the Thomas Fire.

Since the fire, we've had many people call to help, but it is really limited in what people who are not trained to work with the birds can do. We asked if people could bring us lunch. That was a huge help as we were working constantly and this way we did not have to stop what we were doing. So, we had people bringing food. And we had people helping with laundry. We have washers but we usually hang the laundry to dry and could not do that with the smoke and ash, so people would take our clean loads and dry them and bring them back. This was a huge help as well.

We don't know how the birds will do after this. I called around to a lot of other centers to see if anyone had ever done a study on how the birds' respiratory systems do after a fire like this, and nobody has. So, we don't know how they will be.

People have been giving donations for recovery and we've been able to give back by giving barn owl boxes to members of the community. This helps the owls and the natural ecosystem in the Valley. We are working with the community affected by the fire and will give these boxes for free if people cannot afford the cost. It's a way of saying thank you and supporting others while continuing to help the birds.

Photograph by Nathan Wickstrum
Ojai Valley Land Conservancy

Vaughn Montgomery
Greater Goods
May 10, 2018

I live up in Matilija Canyon and Tuesday, at about 5:00 in the morning, my neighbor came over and said there was a major fire and that we should evacuate considering where we live. My housemate and I came down into town at about noon to get some gas and leave a car here and give it a look in person, and then we knew we were definitely leaving that day. The winds were happening and were going to continue for a few days and we had the opportunity to go up to Quail Springs, the permaculture site up in Cuyama. We could tell the 150 was crazy and that was the only other way out of town. And I didn't want to go towards Carpinteria because that was the way the smoke was heading and I imagined the fire was heading that way, too. We gathered our families and animals and went over the 33 to Cuyama and stayed there for about eight or nine days. We had a little bit of internet connection up there, so we could check up on how things were going. We were on pins and needles because the fire came into the Canyon. Our home did not burn but four or five neighbors' homes were taken out. 50-plus homes were spared.

It was a scary time, but we felt really fortunate to come home and still have a house. The area was still so smoky, and we didn't want the kids here, so they went down to my wife's parents' home in Woodland Hills with the mom and kids of our housemate, and myself and the other dad, we came home and started cleaning up the yard and moved stuff away from the house even though it didn't make any sense. The fire had passed but you're running on adrenaline in a lot of ways.

Right around mid-December a friend of mine called a general meeting here at Greater Goods to just check in—quite a few people in the room had lost their homes—and get a sense of people's needs and what people had to offer. We compiled a list and helped to make some connections and it became a bit of a group therapy night in a way, too. That's when it first started.

My sister teaches at Oak Grove and on day five or six—that first weekend after the fire—she worked with Andrew, a school parent who is connected to Direct Relief, and they coordinated bringing boxes of masks in. They set up shop at Greater Goods on that Saturday after the fire and distributed masks to folks.

Andrew encouraged us to open up a relief fund, as Greater Goods is a 501(c)(3). And to our surprise, with very little marketing and maybe one email being put out, the word got out and $15,000 came in. We put it out that we were receiving funds and receiving applications.

We created an advisory board to oversee the fund and oversee the template for where this money was going to go and how it was going to be handled, as we wanted to be able to offer 100% to people in need and have none go to administrative costs.

The first round, given out on Christmas Eve, happened so quickly. We did it very simply: everyone who lost something received equal amounts. If it's a family of two they get twice as much, a family of three gets three times as much. I think it came to $140 dollars per person which is a pretty modest amount when broken up amongst 40 households. And then another approximately 20 households got wind of our work and they applied and we honored those late applications as well.

We have a great advisory board, with a vast and diverse group of people, and so we have a wealth of experience to help us structure the way we set up the fund and how we allocate money. The idea is that we take half of what comes in each time and give that, right away, to those in need, and half we hold back for future needs that arise. We also now look at applications in a more systematic way.

We want to give to everyone but are now able to give in different amounts depending on need. We've created a profile, four to six areas that we could mark off to be able to correctly give to all those who ask: do they have

Photograph by Deva Temple

insurance or not, do they make above or below a certain amount, do they have a substantial GoFundMe page or not, are they a single parent or a two-parent family, or two people with no kids? It's kind of messy work and kind of strange to be thinking of things so personal in a financial way but it seemed appropriate.

As we hit the end of January, I kept getting this sinking feeling that, while this work is so urgent, at the same time we have no income. Like a lot of businesses in town, we had no income in December and very little income in January. And while we knew how important it was to give back in this way, we needed to make it more sustainable because it's a lot of work.

It was a scary time for Greater Goods and then one of our advisory board members suggested we look for funding to underwrite the work we were doing for the relief fund. That is exactly what happened. We were able to get funds from Direct Relief, and also from a local foundation, that were earmarked specifically for administrative costs. When the foundation money came in I remember calling them to make sure this money was not for the relief fund. They said, no, it is for general use, unrestricted funds. It was very humbling and amazing at the same time, that we were getting the support from our community so that we could support our community.

It has been amazing to be connected to so many of the families who are dealing with everything that has happened and feeling that at least I am doing something. Certainly offering money, but also offering a space to have talks and music and poetry and workshops. I get a lot from that. The energy that has come into this space and the support and the trust that the community has placed in us and this space is incredible. A couple of series that started in January were a compassionate listening series, that offered nurturing and support within the structure of a listening circle, and Phoenix Cycle, a seven-week workshop which culminated with the making of the Mandala.

Unveiling the Mandala was an incredible night and brought up a lot of the emotions that surround the fire. It took a lot of us back to that time, the heaviness of that time and the smoke, and also the miracle that while many homes burned, no one was burned in their home. For how many homes burned and how raging that fire was it is a miracle that there wasn't a major loss of life.

Talking about the fire, reflecting with folks, connecting with people, and doing work in the way of fire relief is a great grounding for anyone who is willing to spend these moments. For me, I have to admit, I have a hard time when people are so thankful—because people are still homeless, and people are still unemployed, people are still experiencing trauma from this event. It is important to remember that the intensity of the need and urgency of the need, that it is still here.

For Greater Goods, it's all in flux and we're adjusting as we go. We are figuring out what the future looks like on this side of our business, the Greater Goods Relief Fund. It's complex, but at the same time you can't help but sense a strengthening of connection and appreciation and a refocus of what actually matters, which is about as healthy a lesson as anyone can get.

Photograph by Dylan Dawes

Photograph by Julia Thomsen
North Highway 33, Los Padres National Forest

Tania Parker
Ojai Valley Land Conservancy
May 1, 2018

Everyone at the Land Conservancy evacuated. This is one of the most amazing things about this fire, it was close to every single person's home in the Valley. It didn't matter where we lived, the fire came close to all of us. We all felt very lucky that we were able to take care of ourselves and our families. Brian, our executive director, did drive into Ojai to rescue the few paper documents and binders and other things that aren't stored on the Cloud. But besides that, we all focused on our personal safety.

Two weeks after the fire we came back, regrouped and started to figure out what happened to the land. The first week we were back we didn't get out much. It was still so smoky. But when it started to clear, we started to head out onto the land. We divided the office into groups of two or three and each of us tackled different preserves and assessed the damage. I went out to the Ventura River Preserve and we hiked the ridges first. Other teams ventured out to the Valley View Preserve trails. We assessed and started to clear the trails.

We have a really good core group of volunteers that helped build most of the trails and they all rallied to help. We had teams going out together so that everyone could be safe. One of the biggest goals for us was to get our trails open as quickly as possible, to make them safe so that people could go out and experience the land.

The second day out I headed up Wills Canyon with a small group. Down on the land it took a while for the fire to pass through so, while it was now two and a half weeks after the fire, there were still flames and smoldering stumps, still smoke and hot spots. We were pouring our water bottles onto small fires and trying to smother them with dirt.

It was oddly beautiful. It was very different than up on the ridges, which were very moonscaped and gray. But through the Canyon the fire didn't spread up into the canopy, so the canopy was still bright green and it looked like there was snow on the ground everywhere. It was surreal, and it was beautiful. And part of the ecosystem. It was really interesting to see, and it was really therapeutic to get out onto the land.

This is why we really wanted to focus on opening up our preserves as quickly as possible, so that everybody could experience this. We knew that the regeneration would start to happen quickly and we wanted everyone to be able to get out there and see it in its burned state.

In terms of the actual fire, we found that our preserves were able to provide really good firebreaks and defensible space for the firefighters as they were able to have those accessible trails to make a line. They made a line on the Ventura River Preserve along Oso Road and another to protect Rancho Matilija. They were able to make a stand across the river, too. The conservation land served as a good buffer.

In hindsight, I think we probably could have had a slightly better inventory of our infrastructure, specifically our trail marker signs and benches. We have all the benches documented but we didn't realize that on Google Earth, things didn't really match up, and so we have some work to do to put things right. A few of our benches burned and many of our signs burned. We actually haven't even started to inventory the trail marker signs. We have all of the donor signs and benches reordered, but we are going to reimagine the trail signs and start with a fresh plan.

We were able to get most of our trails opened by Christmas. Chaparral Crest has some sensitive resources, so we've permanently closed that trial and are seeing where we can reroute that. Wills was the last to open because we had to coordinate getting so many hazardous trees taken out. There was so much chainsawing to do because of so many downed trees blocking the trail. We had to go back with arborists, and we had to get permits to take the hazard trees out and make the trails safer.

While the land is recovering we're still going to have slides and issues when it rains. At least for the next five years or so. Because of this we're putting in new water bars and ways for the storm water to drain better, so it won't degrade the trail. It will be a lot of work in years to come.

I was a kid in the '85 fire here. I ended up studying wildland fires and fuel management in college and my mom thinks I chose this because of the '85 fire. She said for years I wouldn't let anyone have campfires and I knew all the campfire rules when I was four. This was a big deal for me. I think because I had studied this for four years I wasn't as torn up about the fire. The recovering of people's homes... what so many people have lost is devastating. But the land, this we get to watch come back and change and evolve, and know that even though five years is going to feel like forever—five to seven years in the grand scheme of things—it's such a tiny amount of time for this ecosystem to recover. For me, it's just been beautiful to watch. I'm excited to hike out there every day and watch the flowers come back, stumps sprout, seeing everything change constantly. It's really fascinating.

The Conservancy works really hard to give people a connection to the land and let them experience it in all of its states, to give people a way to get out there and enjoy it. That was our biggest effort after the fire: to let people see what happened and let them watch the recovery, be part of it and feel connected to their open space. This is what is really important for us.

Photograph by Nathan Wickstrum
Ventura River Preserve

Travis Escalante
American Mattress Man
May 15, 2018

My wife and I were watching the fire on TV and when it got to Wheeler Canyon, in Santa Paula, I went to sleep, thinking that it would be stopped. My wife woke me a few hours later to tell me that the fire was in Ventura. I went to check on my store first and then drove up the hills in Ventura and everything was on fire. And when I drove to the Harbor View Apartment area I literally watched pictures burn off the walls through the windows of the buildings.

When I got back to Ojai I filled up our vehicles with gas and we watched through the rest of the night. Early the next morning we left Ojai. The 150 was already backed up and so we went up the 33 and over to Bakersfield.

We came back Wednesday and it was so smoky. We were only in town a short time when we got a call from a friend who had heard that we were in for another evacuation and so we packed up and went to my sister's home in Newbury Park.

We were nervous wrecks that night, watching the news, hearing that Saddle Mountain was burning, that the Ojai Valley Inn was burning, that Vons was on fire. There were pictures on Facebook but you really couldn't tell if it was smoke or fire or what was really true with all the stories going around.

I am a minister and remembered that I have a press card so that I can get past roadblocks and into places to administer last rites. I told my wife that I needed to go back to Ojai, that I had to be sure that things were okay up there, and I had to help my community.

Thursday morning I started posting on Facebook that I was in town and I was available to help with whatever anyone needed. I drove all over town, taking videos and posting them on Facebook so that people could see what was actually happening when it was happening. And it started to evolve from there. I put my phone number on the posts and people started calling—could I lock their door, check their animals, pick up packages. I would check their home and send a photo or a video so people knew that it was all okay.

The most powerful experience for me was a woman who called me from back east. Her dad and brother lived in Matilija Canyon and she couldn't reach them and could I make sure they were okay? I drove into the Canyon and was able to take a video of the father and son, with the firefighters behind them. She was so thankful.

I did this for five days, running on adrenaline and my love for this community. I grew up in Ojai since I was six months old. It was incredibly important for me to be able to see what was genuinely happening and to share this with others. It was my way to be of service to others. I felt that I was led by Spirit and it evolved into whatever I could do. I reacted by helping and it felt good. God sustained me the whole time.

Photograph by Angela May

Lisa Isbell
Matilija Veterinary Hospital
June 2, 2018

I had recently downsized to a smaller home, and when the fire started on Monday night I found myself reflecting on that process of deciding what was important to me. It was interesting that I possibly would have to do this even more. Then on Tuesday at Matilija Vet it was business as usual at first, but we soon realized that this fire was big. We have 19 animal cages and we cleaned those out and started to prepare for potential evacuees. We doubled up animals so that we were able to take more in.

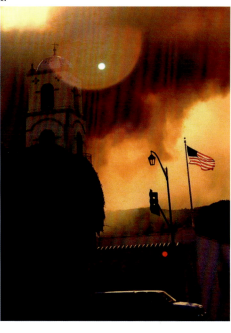

I have friends up on Thacher Road and I went up there and I got their two cats. When I got back to the office there were three other families waiting and we took their cats in, too. Nancy Klimbal and I slept at the office on Tuesday and Wednesday nights, on the benches in our waiting room. And I went back and forth to the East End to water my friends' property for them. I cleaned up leaves and hosed down the perimeter of their land. I wasn't worried about the Valley floor burning—I felt safe in the center of the Valley where our office is—but I knew that their home was at risk.

The animals were scared and we wanted to stay and take care of them the best way we could. We didn't sleep very well but it was worth it to be there. We kept the office open the entire time, and people were coming in the entire time. Some even keeping their appointments even with this fire going on. Dr. Bailey was there through Thursday and then Dr. Bogart took over.

Many people who had evacuated were calling in. They had left so quickly that they did not bring their pet's medication and so we were able to call into veterinary offices all over and give prescription information. It was great that we were available for that.

I went to another friend's home on the East End on Wednesday night. I remember I could feel the heat of the fire. I had a lot of energy still, I was running on that adrenaline, and I hosed down their home as well. The entire neighborhood was gone. It was a very strange feeling to be there like that. But I kept asking myself, *what could I do? what could I do?*, and then did those things that were helpful.

And then on Thursday morning I went back to my friend's home again. I felt exhausted. The other staff at the office kept saying *we need you, you're the only one,* but I went and slept for a few hours and took a shower and regrouped and then I came back to work.

After the fire, I think one of the things that was hard for me was this feeling of disconnect. I felt like we all survived this incredible experience but here it was, Christmas, and so many people had lost so much. It felt so weird to exchange gifts. I donated a lot.

After the fire, when people came in, it was sad but it was good to make contact with those people. A lot of our clients from Upper Ojai lost everything. It was so hard to see them and hear their stories but it was so important. And now we are six months later and it's still so raw. And so it is still good to talk about it. There was—and still is in certain ways—this feeling of letdown. There was so much emotion and everyone came together and now there is often this feeling of *did this really happen?* You know it did but there is this emptiness and this loss that still lingers. And you contrast this to the way our land looks. The mountains are so green.

It is good that this book is being put together; it helps to give meaning to this experience—how people from all different walks of life and in all different capacities came together during this fire. We are strong together. This fire made our community stronger and showed us what it means to be human.

Photographs by Gail Mortensen
December 5, 2017 and May 3, 2018

Cassidy Linder
Ojai Arts Exchange
April 14, 2018

I live about a quarter mile from Camp Ramah so I knew that there was a great chance that I was going to lose my home because of where the fire was. We were going to stay on the property with our landlord and the neighbors and band together. We thought, *we are going fight this fire together if it comes down*, but I was having this intuition that this was not okay, that we were not safe.

We called our landlord, and he said that the hill above Camp Ramah was on fire and that they were leaving. We went to the window and the whole hillside was aflame. It wasn't like a patch. It was from one end to the other. The Santa Ana winds were picking up at this point and we were later told that if the winds had blown south, it would have hit us in minutes.

We packed up as much as we could. I took our laundry because I knew these were clothes that we wear and we got in our cars and drove to our business. It is closer to the center of town and surrounded by other businesses and we felt it was safer because it is predominately made of brick and tin. We took all the gear and put it in the center of the floor and grabbed a couple of buckets of hard drives and as many of Bernie's guitars as we could. We loaded both cars and started to head out. I called my dad, who lives in Santa Paula, and he offered his place as a safe zone, which I know makes no sense since that is where the fires started. Santa Paula was still burning but my stepmom is a pilot and they built an apartment in the airplane hangar. We went and stayed with them. Rescue helicopters were using the Santa Paula Airport as a takeoff point and I felt if they were there then we were safe.

I remember being totally glued to the TV for days, and I couldn't think about anything else because there was this *holy shit my house is probably burned* thought. And the *what would you do if you lost everything* thought. And then the *what could you do if you didn't lose everything and you know people who did?* I had a friend in Ventura who lost her home and another friend, in Ojai, who lost his home, and I'm starting to get these phone calls or I am seeing posts on Facebook of all these people who I know very personally who lost everything. This same day, I learned that my home was safe. Once I felt this relief, I continued to ask myself what I could do for people who lost their homes.

I'm a small business owner who has no savings. We launched our business less than a year before the fires started and it's taken everything to keep it up and running. I don't have any money to give to someone, so what can I give? And I can't just give to one person when so many are in need. I remembered that I used to do these clothing swap parties, where you clean out your closet, swap clothes, and you have a whole new wardrobe.

So I thought, *what if I host a clothing swap?* People could come with items from their closet and those who need can take whatever they want. I

Photograph by Elizabeth Rose

hemmed and hawed over it for about a day and talked to Bernie. We decided to do it that following Tuesday, because we knew that by then it would be safe, and I naïvely thought everything would be back to normal.

I put up a post on Facebook: Clothing swap, time and place. I got a lot of responses and thought *okay, this is going to be really good*. I was under a very naïve impression that by Tuesday everybody would be back to town and we could do this. But when we went back, it was apocalyptic. The sky was beige. The sun was a bright orange. It looked like there was snow everywhere. And everybody was walking around with a mask on. Sunglasses, bandanas, anything to cover. And it was snowing ash.

Tuesday came. I had gotten calls from some people that really wanted to contribute to the event but were out of town and asked if I could pick up items from their homes. So, during the day I was going around and picking up bags of clothes. I had a couple of girlfriends that offered to volunteer and help. I think there

were about five of us working the event and I remember that night it got really windy and cold. People were walking sideways because the wind was pushing them as they dropped off donations—and there was all this ash. The next thing I knew, we had over 30 people donate.

We had over a thousand pieces of clothing. It was remarkable! It was really overwhelming because everything was coming so fast, and we were trying to organize and fix it and create a space so that when the people came it would look nice and be a good experience for all these people who lost everything. We didn't want them to pick through bags. We wanted them to feel a bit of normalcy, as if they were at a store.

So many people donated and not just clothing. I had car seats, TVs, a full comforter set, a ukulele... So many people gave so freely. There was one woman, who had lost her home, and she brought a few pieces in with her that she had taken when she packed to leave. She took things that she needed but she also donated. It was so beautiful. It was this magnificent, amazing gesture.

Russell Kun
Evergreen Wellness
April 18, 2018

There was a guy in a Jeep when I went to the gas station across from Vons on Monday night. I pulled the nozzle into the tank and the power died. And when I said something about it, this guy said he just came from Upper Ojai. He said he had never seen fire move so fast before and that he was getting out of here.

Tuesday morning at 6:00 am I finally got gas and we packed up our two cars. My wife grabbed mementos and legal documents and clothes. I grabbed all the guitars and tequila. And, with two other families, we caravanned out the 150 to Carpinteria. We were at a coffeehouse at 7:15 in the morning trying to figure out which way to go. The people we were with had connections to a hotel in Santa Barbara, so we were there for two days when the ash began to fall from the sky in Santa Barbara. We then decided to head farther north to San Luis Obispo. The hotels in San Luis Obispo were taking in so many people from Ojai they began calling it "SLOjai."

I came back to Ojai on Friday and I put out a notice on Facebook that if anybody needed anything they could just come into the office. Even if they had never been seen before. Anyone, whoever it was, first responders and anyone who was affected by the fires could come. Over 50 people came that day. They came for adjustments and also were able to get masks.

The mask situation was dire. I had heard this before I came back into town, so I loaded up at a San Luis Obispo Home Depot and brought back cases with me. I was blown away by the ash and smoke. I went back to SLO for two days and then put my wife and kids on a plane to New England to stay with family until the air cleared. The kids' school closed a week earlier than it was supposed to so they had a two-week break. And then I came back to Ojai.

In two weeks I was open again. I saw my regular clients and still continued to treat, for free, anyone who had lost their home or had been adversely affected by the fire and all first responders. I continued to do this through the month of January.

Our town is amazing. You could see that we were doing something that other towns and communities were not doing. Yes, there was stress but there was this incredible amount of support. Everyone in Ojai had this one question in their mind, *how are we going to give help?* To give in this way, under this intense stress, to be of service, this was incredible. I could see that the community has a love and compassion for one another. That we have each other's back.

Photograph by Deva Temple

Sheila Louise Piala
Rancho Inn
April 17, 2018

Monday night I went to sleep, and then the phone started ringing and I wondered who would be bothering us at this time of night. When I finally answered the phone, it was my daughter, who lives in Oak View; she and her husband own Ojai Pizza, and she said, *Mom, you have to get out of there, you've got to leave.*

Still on the phone, I woke up my boyfriend and we went outside and looked, and I said to my daughter, *no, we're fine, we're fine,* and we waited until the morning. My boyfriend got a call to go to work that next morning and said, *Sheila, I think we're really going to be fine.*

At this time, you just saw the glow and because I am downtown and work at Rancho Inn which is also downtown, I stayed. Both Monday and Tuesday the hotel was still open, and then on Tuesday it was decided that the hotel would evacuate. At home Wednesday night I realized, *oh my god, this really isn't safe,* and so I went over to the Rancho Inn, and stayed in the back room because it was by the pool where I felt safer. I have bad night vision and cannot drive at night and so I stayed back there. Of course, my neighbors had evacuated. Everyone I knew had evacuated, and Kenny, the owner of the hotel, was calling and asking me to please leave, to go to Santa Barbara. But I stayed at the Rancho Inn. When I woke up Thursday morning, it was one of the strangest things in the world. There was no one anywhere. There was just smoke and glow and ash.

I got in my car and I drove to my parents, who live in Camarillo, and I stayed with them for a bit, but the news was so horrible I knew I had to get back to Ojai. And we reopened the hotel because people needed a place to go.

The hotel had been closed for three days, Tuesday through Thursday. We reopened on Friday. Everyone who works in the hotel lives in Ojai, and so our housekeepers all came, our maintenance guy came, and we just did everything we could to get the property ready for guests. Luckily, we didn't

Photograph by Erin Parker

have any of the smoke damage that everyone else had.

Kenny also owns the Capri Hotel and the Hummingbird Inn, both located in Ojai. And so, while we were getting the Rancho Inn ready, we also opened those two hotels. There was nowhere for the firefighters to stay, and so Antonio, our regional manager, got on this right away to find out what we had to do. You were not allowed to comp anything for the firefighters. Ventura County would not accept comping because our tax dollars pay for this. Antonio got a hold of the State and asked what he had to do to get those guys in here. He explained that he had these two hotels, a combination of approximately 60 rooms. Finally, he got permission, and we filled the Capri and Hummingbird with firefighters. And again, since all the people who worked in the hotels live here in Ojai, we were able to cater to all those firefighters.

The Rancho Inn was filled mostly with people who had lost their homes, or people who couldn't go back to their homes yet because it wasn't safe. There were Rose Valley people, and a lot of people from up beyond Foothill. That whole ridge was still in danger, and a lot of people, even though they had not lost their home, needed shelter because they were not allowed to go home. Others could not stay because of the danger and the ash. Those people would come to the hotel to sleep and then they would leave during the day, if they were allowed to go back to their home.

I was working really closely with HELP of Ojai. There were many people that could not pay and HELP of Ojai was helping pay for rooms. And we were also able to lower our rates. Because we had the other two hotels filled with the firefighters, we were able to lower our rates or comp people completely at the Rancho Inn. Otherwise we would have gone bankrupt, but instead we were able to give back.

Amazing people stayed with us. Beautiful people who had lost everything. People who had humor, people who struggled to feel hopeful and people who were like rays of light. Everyone had lost something. There was a lot of discussion going on about things, the unimportance of them.

It is so hard to explain the experience. It is so hard for people to understand about the fire and after the fire and the damage to the land. And the responders. How they just do it; how they won't take anything from you, even if you want to give it. And so you say, *thank you, thank you, thank you for saving our town.*

I just have to say, what an amazing community Ojai is. We really pulled together and made it less painful. And ridiculous Mother Nature—look at what is happening. I kept saying *the ash is fertilizer, the ash is fertilizer, it will come back,* and then spring's rebirth came and it's like, *are you kidding me? This place is magical.*

Photograph by Garth Rose

Jayn Walter
HELP of Ojai
April 19, 2018

HELP of Ojai was open every day of the week during the Thomas Fire. Staff delivered food boxes to clients, transported folks as necessary and fielded phone calls. The Community Assistance Program office opened Friday morning and distributed fresh food, water, masks and pantry boxes.

We weren't quite sure what the needs would be after the fire. I reached out to agencies that supported the Northern California communities affected by the fires there. They were so helpful in sharing their best practices. I adapted and modified their processes to be appropriate for Ojai.

As a food pantry, we already had resources in terms of food. Donations began to arrive, ranging from clothing to canned food and water and so many other things. These were delivered to our West Campus location which is off Baldwin Road.

And then we started receiving funding. So many people wanted to give. Some people gave to our general fund, while others gave to us in the name of fire survivors. These funds allowed us to create our Phase One fund.

Phase One ran until January 19th. The deadline was based on when the fire was totally put out. It gave us a timeline and a structure for immediate funding. Phase One supported anyone who had been affected financially, so, anyone who experienced financial hardship or home loss.

People came to our Fox Street office and completed an application that looked very similar to our traditional intake and which allowed them to identify areas where they needed support, such as food, legal aid, clothing, housing. We were able to direct them to specific resources. In addition, based on whether they had evacuation costs or lost income, or medical costs including if they lost medication in the fire when they had to evacuate, we could reimburse them.

Eligible Phase One applicants received a flat grant. The purpose was to give immediate funding to those that had been affected by the fire. We gave grants to every verified applicant who lost their home in the fire. We issued grants to those people who had to close their businesses during or after the fire and to the employees of those businesses. Economically there was a significant portion of Ojai who were affected by the fire. They might not have lost their homes, but these folks were still suffering.

Even after we wrapped up Phase One, the immediate need phase, if there were people who still came in and who had significant challenges, we continued to work with them in the same way. Phase One wrapped up close to the time FEMA became involved.

In Phase Two, our priority shifted to housing because we knew that was a significant issue for those who had lost their homes. In terms of funding, we helped people who needed rental assistance; first month and a security deposit. And we also purchased trailers. The motto we stood by through all of this was to replace like with like. We had to really assess what each person's situation was prior to the fire and then determine how we could replicate it. We can't rebuild a home, but for renters, or people living on properties in a fifth wheel trailer, we were able to replicate that.

What is appropriate for one person is not necessarily appropriate for another. What is the best solution for one family is not necessarily what is best for the next and so we looked at what was unique for the individual. This is important for us as an agency and as a community program in general, we always look at people as individuals.

We worked with the Human Services Agency, Salvation Army and Red Cross and referred clients based on their individual needs. We hoped that people would come and sit and talk about their experiences and needs at the time. I think the challenge for so many people was that they did not feel comfortable talking about it. But it is so important, we wanted to know each person's story and we wanted to help.

We also felt this responsibility to be advocates for the Ojai community in what had happened with home loss. It was very different in Ojai. You had a lot of people who were second building or third building dwellers on one property, so in some areas that burnt there could be 15 people. I do not think that people are aware of or understood this. But in one address we are talking about several families. As an agency, we worked very hard to collect information so that we could support everyone on the property.

There were still many people who had not connected to us or are just starting to connect to us now. I think they may have felt that they were okay, and now have found themselves in a situation that didn't work out the way they thought it would.

We then moved to Phase Three. Whereas Phase One was for anyone affected by the fire, Phase Two and Phase Three were strictly for those that lost their homes. And whereas Phase Two was addressing specific housing needs, Phase Three was again, a cash grant.

Everyone is in a different position and only they can decide what their specific needs are. And we wanted to give a grant with that understanding. For one person it may be to pay rent; for another, to purchase clothing; for another, groceries or rebuilding their home.

I have met so many wonderful people who I probably would have never met, who would have never come into our office. I would have never learned the things that I learned about them, their lives and how long they've been here, and it has just been really beautiful how many people trusted our agency through this. It has been a lot of responsibility and also really incredible work. And, whether it was a donor, whether it was somebody throwing an event for us, or someone in need, we heard over and over again that they knew that we would do the right thing. They trust us and trust what we're doing. People came to us early because they knew who we are, and they knew that we would help. And that is simply incredible.

It is hard work. There are days where you see people and they are doing really well and then there are days where these same people cannot catch a break. Everything seems to be going wrong for them. I am just really thankful that I have been able to help.

This experience has been one of the biggest projects I have ever been involved in and one of the most important things I have ever done. I don't think, in any other circumstances, would I have been able to be given this opportunity to help so many people in this way. For me, this is huge, and I am so proud of it. When we rolled out Phase One and put the actual application out there for people it was this incredible feeling that our tiny team has done this, and that our community had given us the ability to do this. To donate and support in this way.

Photograph by Alan Gilliam

THOMAS 500 – POPPY EDITION
✐ Cláudia Figueiredo

It started that first night. I texted my husband in the dark to warn him as he was driving from Ventura, *have you seen this fire?* Power was out so in the dark I started packing to evacuate. We never did. Greg works at the Humane Society and that Monday was the first of several nights he spent there. Days and nights I remained at home, alone with our dog and my fear, trying to make sense of the danger we were in. This was the first of the several nights I slept in my clothes, shoes and glasses, ready to run if needed. But I can't run and I don't drive. I can't understand police scanners that were essential to understanding where the fire was and where it was going during the first hours and days. I'm one of those people who gets lost coming out of an elevator, so I had little idea of how near or far the fire was. For many days I felt alone and scared, in our living room. I felt profoundly powerless and completely useless. I remained like that for many days—weeks, even. The feeling grew, as the adrenaline pooled without an outlet to be released.

Early on, I knew I wanted to crochet. It was a way to occupy my mind and hands and perhaps bring something whimsical to those affected by the fire. I looked for ideas and for patterns, without luck or inspiration. On December 13th, I found it! Jessica Morey Nelson, all the way from Texas, offered crocheted Matilija poppies to whoever wanted them here in Ojai. I began crocheting her pattern. A month later I completed 100 poppies and was ready to stop. But in a little exchange with Trevor Quirk a friendly competition began. We'd race to 500! His goal: to raise 500k for fire survivors' relief. My goal: crochet 500 poppies! About a week later, my husband joined the race by pledging to gather 500 tools.

At the time of this writing, I have completed 275 poppies. Matilija poppies are, for me, a symbol of strength, resilience and beauty. The crocheted ones have given me a bit of purpose. I gift them to whoever wants one. I cannot begin to grasp the sense of loss and grief that individuals and families are going through. We didn't lose anything in the fire. Our home was okay. Our pet was okay. The fear and stress were real, though. Palpable, and in some ways, it lingers till today. And these poppies keep me connected. I hope they bring something positive to everyone who receives one. It's my way of saying, *I care about you.*

Photograph by Elizabeth Rose

Although we lost our home and nearly all of our material possessions, we know that we are rich in family, friends and community. Our hearts are overflowing from the love that we have received and continue to receive. It is a gift that we will always cherish.

Photograph and writing by Dawn and Dana Ceniceros

Alex Kim
Managing Director
Ojai Valley Inn
July 9, 2018

I have experience dealing with hurricanes. I have been running the Ojai Valley Inn for four years. Before this I was running a hotel in the Bahamas. With hurricanes, you deal with having no power and no water. With fire, the smoke and the soot and the cleaning—this is a completely different experience.

Monday night, at 5:30–6:00, we visibly saw fire from the mountains and we began to monitor the news. Our emergency procedures immediately kicked in. We notified our guests of the fire via a letter to each guest room as we waited to hear if we would have a voluntary or mandatory evacuation. And at 4:00–5:00 on Tuesday morning, as the fire was getting worse, we saw on the Ventura County Fire Department map that the corner of Villanova's property, located against ours, was under evacuation. We went ahead and evacuated the Inn.

The Inn was at 50% occupancy and many of our guests were leaving on their own even before this time. We went room to room to physically knock on every guest's door. We started the evacuation at 10:30 am and were completely evacuated by 11:30 am.

I was the last person to leave the property. My executive team all went to the El Encanto Hotel, in Santa Barbara. They graciously offered us a board room and we set up a satellite office there. Our reservation team set up a satellite reservation center at the Marriott Ventura Harbor and we were able to continue to communicate with our guests and manage our reservations.

I commuted into Ojai every day, staying at the Inn four to five hours a day. We had our loss prevention team monitoring the property for looting. There was never a problem, which is a great example of how safe Ojai is.

We are very fortunate that the fire did not damage any part of the property, not a single spot. Our only damage was smoke and soot and particle debris. We did not want our staff to clean the hotel because it is a hazardous environment. I believe it was Friday when we hired Servpro. The president of the company's sister-in-law was supposed to have gotten married at the Inn that weekend—of course the wedding wasn't going to happen—and he told us that he wanted to help us. They started right away. They knew that the smoke and soot would continue to come down for a month and they sealed every room and every window before they started to clean. This way the continued debris would not re-enter the hotel once it was cleaned.

We closed the property for the entire month, opening again on January 11th. We canceled all our reservations and reimbursed all our guests. We paid our staff the entire time we were closed. We could not bring them back until the place was safe, but we felt it was important to continue to pay them. A pouring of thanks and gratitude came through.

Many of our guests were very upset because we did not open the hotel right away. Our guests are very loyal to the property—this is a very important place for them and being closed was very difficult for them. It was also devastating for our local businesses because so many tourists stay at the hotel. We worked with the businesses in town and came up with #OjaiLove.

#OjaiLove was a vacation package in partnership with the town of Ojai. It offered discounted room rates at a selection of hotels including the Ojai Valley Inn, additional perks and discounts at restaurants, boutiques and experience outfitters throughout Ojai, and a donation to the HELP of Ojai foundation, which benefited the local families and small businesses affected by the fire. This brought our business community together in a very strong way.

Photograph by Clay White

Gabriella Chesneau
Food Harmonics
April 21, 2018

In December we were still closed on Tuesdays, so when the fire hit on Monday night I spoke to a friend of mine and we felt that we should leave Ojai for the day. We jumped in the car and thought we'd stay the day in Santa Barbara. But when we got there the smoke had already filtered up to Santa Barbara and it was horrible, very difficult to breathe.

We knew we weren't going back to Ojai and ended up going north, finding a hotel in San Luis Obispo that was offering two-bedroom suites for $50 per night for fire evacuees. Some rooms had a couple of families and four or five pets in the room. Most of the rooms were filled with Ojai evacuees who we knew. In all, about 70 people from Ojai ended up there. The hotel was amazing; they threw us a party one night, a poolside BBQ, with food, beer, wine and live music. It was an incredible act of generosity. An astoundingly beautiful offering.

The next day I went to the hotel's office and asked to speak to the person who owned this incredible place. A woman came out and I started to tell her how thankful I was, and she made it seem as if it were the most ordinary thing in the world. She was so clear that this is just what you do in a situation like this. She didn't seem to even acknowledge that her act was one of kindness.

When I came back to Ojai, it was just me and one chef. I wanted to open the restaurant. I wanted people to be able to get food. Even if it was a limited menu. So, the two of us opened up and we made food. Around noon, I got a call from someone saying, *there is a relief center set up in Upper Ojai and if you want to help, I'm sure they would love food.*

We started making healthy salads and soups. I drove them up to the relief center, and we put a sign in our store window saying we were feeding

first responders and firefighters for free. But that was just a small offering and virtually no one was in town to eat the food that we were making.

I remember having a moment, feeling really unsure and overwhelmed about what to do. Stay open? Keep taking food to Upper Ojai? Close down? Leave town? And then I had one of those Eureka! moments of clarity, where all I know myself to be, my commitment to a spiritual path, all that I believe in about life seemed to burn away my confusion. I heard this inner voice that said, *you own a restaurant, you have the capacity to feed this entire community. That's what you do.*

It was a foreshadowing. This whole experience started with my being at this hotel with this woman who would not even let me thank her while she gave in this most natural way. I remembered that, and took that with me, and gave to my community that was hurting. And in that moment, I knew we had to go all the way.

Food Harmonics has a clear vision and a mission to serve nourishing, healing, only organic food of the highest quality. All of the ingredients together are chosen to bring the body into balance. And that's just at the food level. The environment is also crafted to help the rest of our senses come into balance, as is the training of our staff to serve with love and kindness.

We started feeding everyone for free who had lost anything in this fire. We didn't ask for proof, we just opened our doors and did it. We put a sign in the window and our offer spread by word of mouth. We did this until January 31st and we fed many, many families who came in to eat. And they in turn nourished me and my staff immensely. Gratitude was flying around the restaurant; it was so beautiful to be a part of the many tears and the many hugs.

For me personally, the fire gave me a good look into myself and my life and I realized that I had not been doing enough. Not just related to the fire, but in my life as a whole. That there is so much more I can do, and there is so much more we can do as a community to be kind and giving and help those in need. I think the fire helped me see that through this business I want to give back—in a bigger way, a more humanitarian way. It is not enough to do what I had been doing. I can't go back now that I have had this experience and clarity in seeing what is possible with what we have been given in life.

Photograph by Kerri Sengstaken

TRANSFORMATION BY FIRE OF THE SANCTUARY MUSIC STUDIO

My home away from home.
Project of the last eight months.
Container of my most valuable possessions.

It's wild to have so many things lost in a single swoop.
I lost just about every instrument I own
—except both my upright basses
and some very special 'information'

but for the moment
I feel inspired to create and transform.

I am vividly thankful for life.
Thankful for community.
Thankful for family.
Thankful for friendships.

~ *Oliver Newell, 'Oliwa'*

Photographs by Oliver Newell, 'Oliwa'

Fabien Castel
Ojai Vineyards
April 20, 2018

It was the first time in my life that I faced a natural disaster. I realized that I've faced all kinds of things but never a fire, and really never a natural disaster. So for me, as much as for most people around me, including all the staff, Adam, and the Ojai Vineyard, it was completely new territory. It first brought an amazing amount of worries and fears. We really understood very early on how bad it was going to be because as we were bottling, we smelled the fire and we knew the geographic situation. We very quickly received information. We knew the wind was going to grow and knew where the fire was coming from. It was coming right towards us.

Even though it was still at this amazing distance, because we knew the forecast was for the wind to pick up, we left. I knew firefighters who very clearly said it was not worth it to stay. I think for Adam, the owner, there was no hesitation, although it was his house, land, winery and everything he owned that was really threatened. He left even though everything could have gone up in smoke.

As the week progressed and as everything unfolded, like everybody else in the Valley, we realized how amazingly lucky we became and how we were prepared to lose it all and did not. The fear, worry and anxiety became this immense feeling of gratitude—first for the first responders, the fire department, for all their amazing outpouring of support and help. And then we were grateful for not having lost the winery and houses—and for our community.

We desperately looked for what we could do. And started to really search. It became very evident that HELP of Ojai was really set up to help, that they had done it for a long time, that they had the organization, and we realized that more than goods and services, what was needed was for them to have money. Then it was much simpler. We could stick to what we know, which was serving wine to people and making them happy. We could raise money and we devised, with HELP of Ojai, to open the tasting room, have everybody come, be served wine and buy wine, knowing that 100% of the proceeds was going to go towards this cause. Then Adam really stepped up even further, saying that he was going to match every donation. He was not just giving the space and the wine, but he was giving personally—and that really showed how overwhelmed he was by this chance, by the luck that he had of not losing his life's work.

For Adam, matching the donation was not too much. It's really what you do. We don't exist in a void, we are always all connected. I know that for him this was completely natural. I did not see him hesitate; there wasn't any question. Matching the donations could not begin to match his gratitude and his feeling of luck. He felt that it was the least he could have done, that we could have done.

The event itself was incredible! It was at the tasting room. It was really important to have it here. The winery is on Creek Road and a little disconnected from the community. All this was so community related, the tasting room was ideal. We are really set up to take care of people and, in the end, it was easy to put the event together. This is what we know how to do.

Tons of people came. People were hugely generous. Then it became evident that this event, it really became more than a fundraiser. It became a place for people to share their stories and all that they had lived through. The emotion was incredibly high. There was a need for the community to come together. It actually felt incredible that we, as a winery and as a tasting room, we could be that meeting point, that place of sharing, that place of healing, that place of even having fun knowing how painful it had been for everybody.

I am so grateful for how many people showed up, how generous people were and how people bought tons of wine. It was unbelievable. The emotion that I feel is because of how I got to witness something so beautiful and so good. Everybody came together. And not just with us. Everywhere. There were many other events, other wineries, other restaurants, so many initiatives of helping—with people and animals, horses—and that's where the emotion comes for me.

At the end, I am so grateful for HELP of Ojai because I am realizing and learning about what they have been doing all along, and now I question how much more I can do to be really actively helping the community on a daily basis and not just waiting for when there is a natural catastrophe.

I witnessed, for the first time, this catastrophe, but at the same time witnessed how good it was for all of us in how we came together in this way. We all felt so rewarded by receiving so much in return.

Photograph by Harvey Rawn

THE VEIL BETWEEN CALMNESS AND TURMOIL
Brian Lisus

A late evening neighbor's phone call necessitated a venture outside to gaze at the surreally distant glow on the horizon, a step away from the borders of normality and mundane offerings of a digital screen.

I look with awe at this soft orange amber light coming from the east, far enough for now, like a wise Sage still to be discovered, tirelessly consuming all in its path. How beautiful, how sacred, if only those flames would consume the inner me; thoughts of a wistful past now transformed into an unknowing future.

I briefly contemplate surrendering everything and for an instant feel liberated from the constraints of form and place, to be left with nothing to defend and uphold to scrutiny. These thoughts never shared. Fortunately, I am overcome with a sudden fondness for surrounding objects, each an interwoven thread of my life's tapestry, a journey still in motion. Although breathing, needing nothing more, instinct takes over and from beneath the layers of hidden consternation I pack into the car my green card, a violin and a viola, heeding this forewarned whisper of what might be.

This could never happen to me, surely? The veil between calmness and turmoil is thin. I settle once again into the fortuitous luxury of a soft bed having satisfied my personality me. An hour later the phone screen alights, the piercing warning signal goes off informing its recipients that a fire is heading towards us. Be prepared.

A few moments of alarm give way, and with no electric power available, I kindle two long forgotten Sabbath candles and give them life, illuminating my treasured violin wood supply. The arduous journey outside from workshop to car continues until all the pieces have haphazardly been placed on the rear seat. Back inside, I lie down once again with one ear open to vulnerability and drift off into a light sleep, maintaining a subtle alertness I'd imagine stray cats experience nightly.

There is a neighbor's knock on the door at first light. I arise and we rush outside. Yes, this is happening, fire approaching on two fronts not that far away now. Gusts of wind twirl with controlled chaos breaking off small branches as they descend graciously to the earth, so unusual for this most tranquil place. The dawn bustle of my steps becomes frenetic, throwing tools into Trader Joe's brown bags, my three bottles of Strasbourg turpentine from France—no longer available from a store anywhere on the planet—and a half-filled jar of an organic farmyard wood primer. The mixture glows in the subdued smoky light, made with refinement longing to be applied to some freshly finished wood.

Car packed, I leave in haste, directionless, just in time before the mandatory evacuation is enforced. The energy of heightened 'now' time permeates my every cell. In some outlandish way the aliveness is exhilarating but I dare not mention that to anyone. A day of drifting finds me reclining on a paradoxically hard and unfamiliar hotel bed as the devastation unfolds on the television, image by image. Lives changed, homes lost, every burning crackle freeing forgotten agonies—but I choose not to go there, into the nature of this dream world.

I have touched the depths of despair many times, learning anew that the suffering is only experienced in realms of thought. Only the mind attaches meaning to those outer symbols. I recall those moments, blessings, gifts from an amiable world offering me more ways to let go. I offer silent prayers to those in need as they remind me that sometimes we walk with nothing, other times with plenty… and both are equally good.

There is a calmness, a lucidity, knowing that more gifts of surrendering who I think I am are only a few steps away. Next time it could be me. I cling to a seldom-found courage, momentarily giving up my narrative, and fully embrace reality, allowing the authenticity to unfold with utmost grace, the fire included.

The wanderers, now homeless, find their way to the hearts of friends, neighbors and strangers, where selfless outpouring abounds and both giver and receiver momentarily touch the oneness.

Photograph by Bernard Glasky
Meher Mount, a section of Meher Baba's Tree

Jorge Alem
Ojai Beverage Company
May 15, 2018

I was home in Camarillo when I got a call from my cousin saying that he and my mom and my aunt were all leaving their homes, and could I come and pick them up. My mom lives on Kimball Road and my cousin lives on Via Ondulando—where most of the houses burned down. My cousin's house did not, he got lucky. My aunt lives near Petit. The fire was going toward all of them. I don't remember the exact time of the call because all the electricity was out and my phone was almost dead; I was trying not to use it too much.

I jolted from Camarillo and as I was driving down the freeway it was almost empty. It was only 9:15 pm at this point, and when I got to Ventura everything was lit up, it was like daylight. You could see everything perfectly because there was so much fire coming over the ridge and going towards Via Ondulando. I got everyone and took them all to my uncle's house in Thousand Oaks. And then the next day I tried to get to Ojai. The 33 was closed and I couldn't get in, so I began making food for the Red Cross and people that were evacuated to the fairgrounds from my restaurant in Ventura. And as soon as they opened the roads I left my staff there and went up to Ojai. I didn't leave until the following Sunday.

Every day we had people coming into Ojai Beverage Company. And we had people spending the night there. We gave them access to the store as a place to stay, and we fed them. The only thing I wouldn't do was give them the beer. I didn't want to influence that. But it was all about giving. I was trying not to be in business. I didn't want to profit off of something so tragic.

A lot of my customers lost their homes. People I have known for a long time through this business, not on a personal basis but still people I knew. It was just a rough time; everyone just needed help.

I have the most amazing crew. They all came in, volunteered their time in making sandwiches for the Red Cross in Ojai, for any customers that walked in, for any orders that we had. We fed so many firefighters, I can't even tell you how many. We did three to four hundred orders of sandwiches. We dropped off at the police station and we delivered to the Humane Society and we delivered to fire crews. A lot of fire crews were sleeping on people's driveways, so we would go and drop off sandwiches because they couldn't leave.

Our vendors were coming up to Ojai through the smoke and dropping off cases of water and supplies. It was really touching. I am not an emotional man, but I was extremely emotional during the fires. This is our town. I remember standing on the roof of OBC, Wednesday night, and the fire was coming over the ridge and we're thinking, *there goes our town*. It was extremely emotional, and it was scary because you can't do anything. You can help people that need help but you can't stop something this massive. I think the firefighters are a godsend. If it wasn't for them Ojai wouldn't be on the map anymore.

I think about this fire often. It was huge, and when your town suffers, you remember. I don't know if it was the same in every town but the amount of support and love that people showed each other was so overwhelming. I think the fire was a blessing for Ojai. I know that may be contradictory to what people think but you have to see light out of dark, and this is what I see. For such a negative thing such positive things came out of it. Amazing and positive things. People pulled together, they rallied together, they put aside their political, their religious, and any other kinds of beliefs and at the end of the day they helped each other.

Photograph by Jasmine Williams

Photograph by Peter Stuart

Tessa Magill
Upper Ojai Relief
May 8, 2018

I had to do something. I heard a lot of people were helping out in Upper Ojai, I had all this time and I knew that there was huge devastation up there. I went up and started sorting clothes and items and ended up being there all the time. And I became a part of the movement up there.

Trevor Quirk and Justin Homze, residents of Upper Ojai, started the relief station. They stayed and fought the fire. They were saving homes for days and days, helping with a lot of houses, with clearing land, with sifting, with creating a place of support for the Upper Ojai community. And Jessica Colborn has been the most helpful person to Upper Ojai residents because she has been physically present to residents since the beginning.

The money we have raised has gone to help Upper Ojai. Roadblock to roadblock is the terminology that was used because there was a roadblock right at the bottom of the grade and then another at Thomas Aquinas, and the goal was to help people within those roadblocks. And we created a running list of names and details. Anyone who applied received funds.

We looked at four details: insured or non-insured, total loss or partial loss. And we posted online and on our website and through word of mouth that we were giving back to our community in this way. Our first distribution of funds was in February and we distributed over $100,000.

We had a barbeque after the fire. It was amazing to get all these people together. It was still a war zone up here. I would go to lower Ojai or into Ventura and things were kind of getting back to normal, but you go to Upper Ojai and it was still a war zone. The oil seeps were still burning, and the smell was so strong. And you could see on people's faces that they were just surviving. There was still so much sadness and trauma and loss.

We are keeping focused right now on trying to stay super relevant and remind people that this Upper Ojai community is still suffering. We have wristbands and T-shirts and stickers that say Upper Ojai Relief, so we stay on people's minds.

A couple of weeks after the fire we had a meeting and asked the community what they want from us, what they need from us, what they are hoping we can become for them. They said they want this station to continue and they want a community center. Years back there used to be a community center where Upper Ojai had parties and bands would play at what is now the Stagecoach Market. The community members have mentioned becoming distanced from each other over the years but now, with the fire, this beautiful thing that has come out of this, people are getting to know their neighbors. People are meeting each other where they hadn't known each other before. There are all these beautiful connections coming out of this disaster. And the people here in Upper Ojai, they are motivated to continue this. To stay together.

Photograph by Trevor Quirk

Painting is a place of peace and escape for me, and it was a natural healing process to be in my studio.
This is how I processed the fire.
I auctioned the paintings and the proceeds were donated to those who had lost so much in the fire.
The good that came from the fire was to witness the love, generosity and true compassion of our small community as we came together to help each other during this trying time.

Many artists living in Ojai confided that they had lost their verve to do their art during and after the Thomas Fire.
The fear and devastation that struck our small valley was too overwhelming.
We all react differently, and mine was the opposite.

I went directly to my easel and painted a series of paintings to document my experience and emotions during that period.
The surreal experience of those weeks in December of 2017 is something that will always be etched within me.
It was as though normal life had stopped.
Angst and the longing to do something to help was the predominant mindset throughout the Valley.

Artwork and writing by Duane Eells

INITIATION BY FIRE MANDALA
⇒ *River Sauvageau*

In the spirit of the Phoenix, which rises from the ashes every 600 years, we offered Phoenix Cycle as a gift with the intention of healing through different modalities. We started with ritual and shared both theatre and therapeutic exercises, had council, and finished with a group Mandala, representing our initiation by fire.

In the north, representing the air, a Raven facing east looks out over mountains covered in swirls of smoke with a blue sky and clouds above. A harbinger of the in-between time when one thing is turning into another, this communal bird has two of her companions flying high above.

In the east, representing the Earth and the beginning, comes a figure walking from the burning mountains. She has smoke all around her body and she comes with animals in her pockets, in her arms and on her head. Mountains burning in the night are to one side of her with a herd of running horses, racing like the fire. Horses are powerful animals and, like the people of the Valley, they have beauty and strength. On the other side the iconic Ojai Post Office tower stands out in the dark smoke. A flying pig above represents the miracle of our downtown saved from the advancing fire by a change in the winds.

In the south, representing fire, a figured fawn stands among honeycombs in patterned figures which go from the earth to the sky, with flowers and bees all around. The fawn appears as a shape-shifter in this otherworldly psychedelic tableau. In true sky above are the head and tail of the Fire Dragon, which is looped around the center of the Mandala and symbolizes the wildfire which circled the Valley all around. In the very center of the Mandala is the universe, with Ursa Major, Ursa Minor, the Pleiades and stars sparkling.

In the west, representing water, the end of the day and the passageway into the Great Mystery, we find a Spirit Bear and Bear Angels, which illustrate the bears that were burned in the fire and who touched the hearts of the people. They are shown in a calm green field with sage plants and a river running down from the mountains.

The Mandala is bordered in white, purple and dark and light green waves—from the white hot feeling of the fire experience moving into the purple of transcendence and integration to the greening rebirth of spring. Life as we know it has its natural cycles, which are ever at play—its up and down rhythms, its changing forms passing from one thing into another.

The surest thing we can know in intense circumstances is that this too will pass and when we live within the passageway with clear intent and support both given and received, each of us personally, as well as communally, are strengthened. This Initiation by Fire Mandala represents the time when we in the Ojai Valley were unified through the Thomas Fire.

Photograph by Elizabeth Rose
The Phoenix Cycle, Greater Goods, January & February, 2018.

Melissa Blanchard
NoSo
May 30, 2018

There was a post about a fire in Santa Paula and my exact words were, *uh oh, we've got another quickie Santa Paula fire.* Because that is what we are used to. Then the power goes out and I am thinking that maybe it's a bigger fire than I thought and maybe it had burned a power line going into Ojai. I went outside and it was so eerie and so windy. I got in my car to check on NoSo. I was worried about the business because we have food and the power was out and so things were likely to spoil. The whole entire town was blacked out. And the trees were swaying and those huge eucalyptus branches were falling all over the place.

I parked in the parking lot and looked up and the sky was just a red glow and tree branches were falling from the wind and I knew I had to go back home. If we lost all of our food at NoSo then we lost all of our food but I needed to be home. There was nothing I could do. I got home but did not sleep.

My family lives on Saddle Mountain, and we have horses boarding there and on Persimmon Hill. *Do we go up there, do we check the horses? What do we do?* It was exhausting and we really couldn't tell what was truly happening and what was rumor. The fire did come up to my family's house, but by that time the firefighters were already there and they stood watch for 24 hours in front of my parents' house. It was ridiculous, the things that they did. They were amazing.

The next day we played it by ear. Because my family was here in the '85 fire they were saying *no we're going to be fine*, and I was saying that I didn't want to be locked in here with the roads all closed. We had all of our dogs and animals and the horses had to be evacuated. A savior showed up on Saddle Mountain with a trailer and tagged our horses and took them to safety.

On Persimmon Hill we got a call: *get up here and get your horses out now.* But we didn't have time. They just opened the gate and said *go guys go!* And the horses didn't move. These were neglected horses that we adopted and they were not very friendly to each other but when we got back after the fire, they were huddled together in the corner of the barn. Safe and scared and connected.

We evacuated to Oxnard and I came up each day to check on NoSo. And then on Monday, one week after the fire started, I came back for good. A few of our customers had reached out, *are you still here? We need somewhere to go to be with our people,* and we knew we had to reopen.

We had the same five people every morning right when we opened. We exchanged phone numbers and became very close friends. We were a community within the larger community that is Ojai, and we would sit for hours together, just to be with each other at this time.

This fire gave us a taste of what Ojai is actually made of, what we actually fight for and why we live here and why we love here and why we raise our children here. We are so blessed and so lucky that we can be part of this beautiful Valley and this beautiful community.

I believe we are still dealing with the trauma of the fire. And while some of the community feels that things are back to normal because we are connected in this deep way, many of us are still struggling and still do not have a permanent place to live and are still financially suffering from the Thomas Fire. We are all, collectively, hurting. That is what I believe. We collectively move together. We are still in this and need to remember to love and support each other.

Photograph by Dylan Dawes

Ernest Niglio
Rainbow Bridge Market
May 1, 2018

We kept expecting more people to come into the store but so many people stayed away for a long time. Because we weren't sure what to order, what to keep on the shelf, or how much prepared food to make we had to throw away a lot of refrigerated items that had spoiled and we lost product due to expiring dates. It took over a month before most people came back to their homes, afraid of the smoke and ash, so sales in the store were slow for a very long time.

      Yet, we kept Rainbow Bridge open the entire time that the fire was active. The people who stayed in town were grateful that we were here. Our kitchen staff continued to make prepared foods for the deli and what we were not able to sell we donated to the firefighters and to the local shelter. And we continued to pay our employees who left town because of the fire. We figured we lost about a quarter of a million dollars because of the fire. We were lucky, a lot of people lost a lot more.

      When you are in the middle of such a large catastrophe you really don't know what the right thing is to do. I figured if I needed to leave during the fire the authorities would have let me know. So I bought air filters and put them all over the store and stayed open to try and do what I could to help. It was a blessing because we fed our community. And that is exactly the right thing.

Photograph by Christina Fortney

Karal Gregory
Ojai Spirit
April 14, 2018

Two days after the fire started, I woke up with this idea of creating a fundraiser. I'd created fundraisers in the past—coffee mugs, things like that—and I thought I would put together a simple mug. I needed a name for it, so a friend and I brainstormed and came up with the idea of Ojai Spirit. I worked on it for three straight days with the intention of using local photographs, but in the end the full-color printing became complicated and expensive. And then I looked into my friend's kitchen, where I was staying during the evacuation, and there were all these mini wine glasses. There were already several T-shirt fundraisers and someone on Facebook joked that they really wished there was a wine glass and I was, like, *Okay, I'm on this one.*

I decided on these nine-ounce wine glasses and I put out a call for someone to help me design a logo. A friend put me in touch with Johanna Bjork. She lives here in town and has a design firm. She came up with a design for me within a matter of days. The first glasses came out right before Christmas. The idea was to get the glasses in hands before New Year's Eve. So, I began taking orders from people online. I ordered 144, sold them all, and ordered another set.

At first, I was just going to do it all by myself, but then I talked with Bob Huey of Point De Chêne Wine and Beer. He was really into the idea and wanted to help, so he let me put them in his shop. Casa Barranca ordered some and they each went through several orders of them. And then Bookends Bookstore ordered them and went through several orders as well. Rainbow Bridge carried them and sold all they had.

We donated half the money to the Humane Society of Ventura County—whose staff and volunteers did an incredible job during the fire—and half went to the Wildland Firefighter Foundation, since so many firefighters live here in Ojai and so many of them from elsewhere helped us. The WFF supports families of fallen firefighters, offers long-term grief recovery, supports injured firefighters and works with long-term trauma effects on the firefighters and for their families. We've donated a total of $2,500 to these organizations so far. We also donated many glasses to Greater Goods and the Porch Gallery. They're donating all profits equally to the Greater Goods Relief Fund and the Thomas Fire Artists Recovery Fund.

Compared to people who had lost their homes, I wasn't really affected by the fire—at least not on the outside. My housemates and I stayed away for a week and came back to a lot of ash and the scarring of our mountains, and that was it. But I woke up early on the third morning in, to an intense anxiety that only now, eight months later, is just starting to subside. Unfortunately at the time, I let it separate me out because I felt I should somehow just be okay, but intuitively I knew it was important to connect with the community. Creating Ojai Spirit helped me to stay connected and grounded and to feel that I was doing something useful that fit my skin.

When people showed up at my door to pick up their orders they were really excited. And I think that represents the spirit of Ojai—people willing to buy something knowing that the money was going to go towards helping their neighbors. It was a very positive kind of embodiment of what the people of Ojai stand for.

Photograph by Elizabeth Rose

When I brought my mobile printing trailer out to an event at Nordhoff, it was one of the proudest moments in my career. Some of my softball players, donning dust masks, along with a few other volunteers, came to help sell shirts. We sold out and took orders and continued to produce more shirts. I can't tell you how much money I lost during that time period because it was the slowest time on my books in thirteen years. I can tell you that the lack of wealth in my pocket does not compare to the riches in my heart to know that many were helped by something I did.

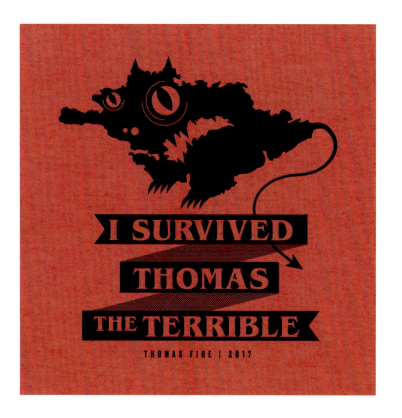

Never have I felt so powerless in the face of such a force. What good I could do was create, to express how I was feeling. As an illustrator I am in a fortunate position of being able to vent through my art. I did just that. I put pen to paper and tried to get out my feelings as fluidly as the ink bleeding from my pen into the paper. When the fires had been backed out of the valley and people began returning, many efforts were being made to give back. Hearing that the Humane Society had done all they could to assist in the housing of the animals left behind by fleeing residents I knew that I needed to do what I could to contribute to their efforts. I drew a simple design illustrating the helping hands surrounding the Valley we all hold so dear. I was able to sell a large number of the shirts to Ojai residents and beyond. It was an amazing outpouring of support. People who only had visited the Valley once before held a place in their hearts for it and wanted to do what they could to contribute.

The Thomas Fire struck home for me, literally. Despite the many messages, phone calls, social media warnings and people straight telling me to get the hell out of Dodge, I stayed. Call me stubborn, and you would probably be right, but I wanted to be a feather on the wing of the Phoenix that would inevitably rise up to lift our town out of the ashes. Ojai is my home, and I can now see the Phoenix rising in its full glory from the ashes. Our valley was tested to its limits. Our community was stronger and neighbors united against the beast by the name of Thomas.

Clockwise from top left: writing by Don Rodarte and design by Don Rodarte and Jeri Washburn, writing and design by Daren Magee, writing and design by Amun Levy

Nicholas Franklin
April 20, 2018

I grew up in Ojai and was here in 2005 when we had the torrential rain and the roads all washed out. Ojai was sealed off. I was fresh out of high school and it was at that time that I realized that there are only four ways out of town so if they wash out you are sealed off.

Now I am a parent and when I saw the smoke I knew we were leaving. Quickly. I didn't want to wait for all these people to be trying to go out the mountain pass at the same time.

We went up to Los Alamos for a night and spent most of our time scrolling through Facebook, which became the best source for information even though there was a lot of misinformation too.

Ultimately, we ended up in San Francisco for six nights. My wife's aunt lives up there and we were able to stay with her. And it all became very weird for me because, while my first instinct was to get my son out of Ojai, there were many guys from my high school class that I was seeing on Facebook and they were all heading into Ojai to help fight the fire. They did really good work and it would have been really nice to have been able to help in that way. But it was not what I thought in those first moments. In those first moments when I saw the smoke all I wanted to do was to get my son somewhere safe. That was my priority.

When I did get back, Ojai Vineyard did the fundraiser for HELP of Ojai at the tasting room. We set up with long, communal tables, so that people could really come together. So many members of the community showed up, including people who had lost their homes. My house burned down in 7th grade; it was a house fire and I understood how people felt. I felt so badly for all these people that lost everything. It meant a lot that we were able to pull everyone together and have this event. And to contribute to such a good organization. Everyone transcended their differences and came together for the betterment of everyone. We came together as a community. This experience did that.

Photograph by Brian Aikens for the Ojai Valley Museum

Bob Huey
Point de Chêne Wine and Beer
May 1, 2018

We took our children and our animals and left at 2:00 am. I came back a week later. I wanted to be here for moral support more than for anything else. I wanted to feel a part of the community and be supportive for those who were here and needed help. I wound up mostly connecting and talking to people. It was still too smoky for people to think about wine.

That first weekend that I was back there was a fundraiser at Ojai Vineyard. I was very grateful to be a part of that. Those guys are such an important part of the community and so integral to the Ojai experience. For them to put up that kind of event meant a lot.

From that point on, my shop was constantly busy. And I think that event kicked it off, because people had a real need to come together and tell their story and tell what happened. I was so glad to be a part of that, often over a bottle of wine.

We participated in a number of fundraisers for Upper Ojai Relief and with Ojai Vineyard. We gave all of our profits from one weekend to these efforts. We wanted to give as much as we could and we had the flexibility to do that. To give in that way meant so much to me. It really shows the strength of our community when people come together and do things for each other. Ojai did this.

And we were able to be involved in Ojai Spirit. Karal came in and asked if I wanted to carry the wine glasses. I love the concept of Ojai Spirit because it is something that continues. The fact that it is an ongoing thing is wonderful; to be able to continue to support this unique community means a lot to me. This is a special and rare place. I am grateful every day to be here.

Photograph by Brian Aikens for the Ojai Valley Museum

Emily Ayala
Friend's Ranches
June 28, 2018

I was at home when the fires started. We just had our big holiday party that weekend and we had a lot of firefighter friends over because my husband is a retired firefighter. Everyone was talking about the big wind event. As farmers we all knew that it was going to get dry and windy. Our trees don't like dry wind, especially in the winter, so we had been irrigating.

On Monday night we saw the glow and started getting phone calls from friends as we watched the fire grow. My husband went to bed, saying there was nothing we could do, but I am the kind of person who worries—if someone is burning toast in the kitchen I am clearing the house—so I watched the glow burn across the whole mountain and then we got a phone call from my husband's best friend who lives in Ventura. They had lost everything.

In the morning the fire was on Dennison Grade which was way too close for comfort for me. Some of our employees showed up at our house, we didn't work that day and they wanted to know what to do and where to go. We had the irrigation going on the edges of the orchards until Casitas Municipal Water District asked the bigger water users to shut their water off because it was needed for the fire.

My husband was watching the fire and said it was going to jump over behind the Thacher School and go into the Topa Topas and there was nothing stopping it. It was so dry and the wind was crazy. We have these big oak trees that were being pummeled and so many big branches were falling as the trees were getting thrashed around. The fruit gets scarred when the branches whip around like that and we were thinking that next year's crop would not look very good. And a lot of our oranges were falling off the trees.

There wasn't a lot that we could do. I packed the kids and the dogs around noon, when the fire crested around Thacher, and we all drove to the Packing House on the 33. We had the water going there and we took our important documents and loaded them into the car. I went to my parents' home across the road and took important records from there, too. And then I drove up the 33 and over the other side. The drive was beautiful.

I wanted to get my kids out. I was getting really stressed and so they were getting stressed, too. We went to Paso Robles where my cousin lives. He's off the beaten path. We didn't have much internet and his phone lines were down for a while due to someone knocking down a telephone pole and all of a sudden I had no connection. It was really hard to leave my husband and now I wasn't able to see what was happening at home. I wanted to get back.

My husband had been at the Packing House. He then went back home and was not able to get back again. He was also just getting bits and pieces about what was happening. On the bright side, we started texting with a group of residents that live near the Packing House that we hadn't really spoken with much before this. We had this great communication going with these people. We created a community. This really brought us together.

The fire blew down Cozy Dell/Sheldon Canyon and then it spread both ways, up and down the riverbed. There was this fairly large stand of eucalyptus trees on the bank of the river and when that went up people in Meiners Oaks could see that huge flame and that really scared a lot of people.

When the fire blew down Cozy Dell behind the Packing House, people sent me pictures and I thought for sure that my parents' house had gone. I was listening to the scanner and it was really scary as I didn't know what I was going to come back to. By Friday, I couldn't stand to be away anymore and I came home. Our house was fine, as was my parents' home; I didn't know this until I got back.

There have been four fires behind the Packing House in my lifetime. Every 10 to 15 years on that north hillside, so the fire didn't burn as hot or as hard because it burned more recently.

On the photo of the Packing House with the fire behind it you can see that the light is on which meant that the electricity was on. This meant that we still had water and that is what saved us. If the fire had come from the other side and burned our well and our electrical lines we wouldn't have had any water and this building would probably have burned down.

The really scary part to me now is the mudslides. We live in a mudslide prone area—the first packing house my grandfather built washed away. For the next four years we are going to have a real threat in this valley of mudslides and there is a lot less you can do about a mud flow than a fire.

This fire is kind of a relief because every day for the last ten years I would look at the hillside behind the Packing House, especially when it got windy, and hope that nobody was smoking. We have so many more hikers on the Cozy Dell trail and I have found piles of burned sage on the rock and it just kills me. I hike Cozy Dell fairly often and I always take that sage ash and get rid of it, it's just a terrible thing to do because it only takes one spark. And so it's kind of a relief that we have all this burnt. Until time builds up the brush again. For farmers that have land against the edges we are always clearing brush. If we have a free afternoon that is what we do. And so it's safer now. But only for a time. Even though it is risky and can get out of control, I wish we did control burns. Because it will happen again so be prepared. It's fire. It's Mother Nature.

Photograph by Maeve Juarez

The awe inspiring power of the Thomas Fire was one of the most devastatingly beautiful events I've ever witnessed. The wind swept flames that rapidly surrounded us eventually revealed contours of the mountains like a reclining nude exposing her beauty. Impressive were the pyro-cumulus clouds towering into the stratosphere like monumental castles to the sky, and at its feet the vigilant stronghold of a tight-knit community.

Inspired by the many handmade signs thanking fire crews and first responders, I wanted to create a banner acknowledging the citizens of Ojai by depicting a phoenix rising from the flames. With spray paint, markers and fallen ash I worked on the ground under the glow of an amber sun.

Artwork and writing by Domonic Dean Breaux

BBQ
Brenton Butler

I experienced the Thomas Fire through a cell phone screen and the windows of my barbershop. The town during the fire was a haunted, lonely place. A ghost town, though the tumbleweed had succumbed to flames. I opened my shop as soon as I could, four days after the fire started. I was in San Diego the night the fire started. My partner Juju and I decided to return.

The drive into Ojai was a chilling one. As the smoke plume grew larger so did my apprehension. Opening the barbershop during the fire provided normalcy, for myself and others. Clients and friends would stop by, take off their masks, and tell their stories. We would act as though everything was fine, but everything had a different smell, taste and hue during the fire. At once alien and familiar.

My friend and BBQ expert, Gordon Branchaud, contacted me about throwing a BBQ in the barbershop parking lot to provide food for the firefighters and any family in need. He told me he wanted to do something, had to do something, and had a freezer full of meat. Smoke from the Thomas Fire and smoke from the grill intertwined. Friends came out and we shared experiences, hugs, food, beer and cheer. It was nice to socialize and be around other people. It was nice to pretend it was all okay.

The people who stayed in town during the fire all wanted to do something to help; everyone was trying to offer something. We offered free haircuts to first responders and those who had lost their homes. The firefighters kept us busy and we made new friends in the process. Grateful and giving, firefighters from all over the United States made us feel safe and truly at home. Serving them was an honor.

BELONGING

Our spirits were awakened through service to others.
We were shown that we were not alone.
We now belonged to a sacred group of survivors

Amanda Colon Rogers

Photograph by Jasmine Williams

Crow Lauren
May 3, 2018

I did not want to get trapped. We knew there was a fire and it was growing pretty rapidly. Clare's sister had gone through the Santa Rosa fire, and knowing her experience, along with how fast this fire was growing and the fact that we live in the Canyon, which only has one way out, we were pretty worried. We were using a generator for power and going online for short amounts of time to keep track of what was happening. And soon we decided we needed to leave.

We grabbed our computers and our cat. And I looked around thinking *I love that thing* and *I love this thing*, but I was not able to take it all and I couldn't choose. I couldn't deal with choosing. So I left everything.

We drove to Goleta. It was pretty intense driving past Lake Casitas because the fire was already at the other side of the lake and the way the road turns it looked like we were driving into it.

At some point we heard that four houses in our area were fine so we thought that we were okay. We had this deep sense of relief, but then the next day one of the neighbors was able to get in far enough and we learned that our house didn't make it.

I cried like somebody died. Our house had everything we owned in it. All of our business tools and our supplies and inventory, and all of our personal items. And we had hand built this house over the last two years. Everything we had was lost.

I had no idea, at first, what to do. I thought I was ruined. I didn't have a job because I had left it to work on our business. And Clare did childcare and that dried up because everyone who had kids and was able to leave, left, so there was no work.

My sister started the GoFundMe page. I was traumatized and couldn't think what to do. And that made me cry over and over again. It was touching and amazing to realize how much community support there is and was at the time. The Ojai community was so very generous and caring, and I felt that I was able to connect on this deep heart level with so many people. People who I knew and people who I had just met because of this fire.

We were offered a guest house, which was really amazing. A woman who we did not know heard we had lost our home through a mutual friend and she texted me. She said that she had this guest house and we could go look at it and if we liked it we could stay. It was this beautiful space and they just offered it to us in the most generous way. There were these beautiful oak trees and everything was clean and spacious. It was such a quiet and good place for us to heal from the trauma because it felt really safe and contained. We stayed for four months. We felt so grateful and lucky that she reached out.

HELP of Ojai helped us purchase an Avion trailer. They are amazing; Jayn is incredible. The organization is so thoughtful in all the different aspects of how they communicate with people. I found them to be very elegant and graceful in the way they reached out and helped.

I think one thing that definitely happened for me, and I think for Clare too, was that when all our material possessions were taken away, and also our way of life—the fact that our business was in our home, and that we were so connected to this one place, to the house and also to the land—when it was all taken away there was this sudden shift of everything. At first I thought *oh, I have to rebuild it all*. But how I relate to material objects that are part of my life has changed. What seems like yours really is not. And I realized that I get to bring forward into this new creation of this new life what is most important. Fire is a cleansing medicine and it is important to look at this opportunity to choose what is coming forward into this new life we are creating.

We didn't financially recoup everything that we had but it doesn't really matter. We were very graciously supported by lots of different people and organizations. And now we have the ability to choose how to craft our life. I know that, while it was traumatic, I just feel that we were really, really lucky and really fortunate. I feel excited about what we are working on. Whereas before I would stress out about what I was working on, now I am being very careful about how I spend the hours of the day and what I carve time out for.

Watching how amazing it was that other people gave in such a profound manner makes me feel like I want to give in that way. Giving is part of a cycle, and I think it has inspired me to be less individualized in my view of how the world works and to open up more to a kind of connected social web of life.

Photograph by Simone Noble

As 50-foot flames engulf Black Mountain, I notice a tall dead sycamore tree in the creek behind our home.
Sitting in the branches are a hawk, two crows, a dove and other small birds.
They are all watching the fire destroy their home. It is a prolific statement from nature.
In the face of danger, all came together and sat in harmony.

➢ *Debbie Armond*

We will heal from this and the land will heal. We can never replace what has been lost—not the houses nor the pieces of people's lives that lie in ashes, not the animals who ran but didn't make it, nor the plants that offered themselves up when their time came. We can only allow ourselves to feel the enormity of this loss, moment by moment, heartbeat by heartbeat. Draw close to those you love no matter how far away we are.
In the end, I believe we all know this, love is the only thing that really matters.

➢ *Deva Temple*

Photograph by Lori Hansen

Photographs by Brian Aikens for the Ojai Valley Museum, OBC photograph by Julia Thomsen
Opposite page: photograph by Nathan Wickstrum, Ventura River Preserve

Celebrating Regrowth

WILLS CANYON IN THE TIME OF FIRE
Zoe Murdock

In the days before the fire, Doc and I ran the trails in Wills Canyon almost every afternoon. We ran other trails around the Valley too—Cozy Dell, Pratt, Foothill, Shelf Road, Sulfur Mountain Road—but Wills Canyon was always our favorite. We could go out our front door, run up the road to where we could drop down into the river valley, hop across the river, rock to rock (when there's water), then up into Wills Canyon. We'd been running up there for years before the fire came. We knew every hill and valley, every root and rock.

After all those years, we were well known to the coyotes and the deer, the mountain lions and the bears, and that funny little skunk that waited in the same spot with her tail up. I tried to scare her off, but when she wouldn't scare I decided to race past her as fast as I could. That's when I found out it was all a ruse designed to make my run a little more fun and exciting.

There were days when we'd see black rattlesnakes coiled up, mating. They were oblivious to us, so we just ran on past them. On hot days, sometimes the biting flies would swirl up in six-foot-high columns, so thick we'd have to close our eyes and dive through them. Either that, or turn around and go home, which was never an option.

On hot summer days, we'd run late so we could catch the cool breeze after the sun went down. That's when we'd hear the sound of big wings pushing air, followed by the distinctive cry of an owl. Many evenings there'd be a whole chorus of birds in the canyon: ravens and crows, little tweety birds, and chirpers, coupled with the loud hum of the bees that lived in the hollowed-out tree up near the gate into the Los Padres National Forest.

On the way back down we'd break out of the trees and head across the meadow, where there was always a different sky waiting for us. Often it would be a pure blue sky with a golden glow over the hill where the sun had gone down; other times the sky would be stretched with pink cotton-candy clouds, maybe with a pale yellow moon floating high above Topa Topa.

Then the Thomas Fire came. We heard it was burning over near Santa Paula. It wasn't long before we heard it was burning up houses in the foothills of Ventura, burning up all the trees in Arroyo Verde Park, where Doc and I both held age-group records in a cross country race that is known as the toughest in Southern California; a race we'd just run a few weeks before.

Even as the fire began to encircle Ojai, blown by winds from the east and the south, we thought the firefighters would put it out and we'd be okay. It never seemed possible that it could burn all the way to Wills Canyon. But it just kept going and going, and pretty soon it had burned across the face of

the mountains to the north, and then it jumped Highway 33 at Cozy Dell and moved down into the river valley, burning some houses there. The air of Ojai soon filled with so much smoke and ash, it was hard to see across the road.

The power went out; no cell phones, no TV, no internet. It was as if we had lost all connection to the outer world. That was the most anxious time

Photograph by Zoe Murdock

for me. I was afraid there'd be a knock on the door in the middle of the night telling us to evacuate, and we wouldn't have anything ready. I didn't know what I needed ready. I just wanted to be ready. I wanted to do something. But what?

We were pretty sure the house would be okay. But what if the air filled with so much smoke we couldn't breathe? What if we couldn't get out of town then? Once the fire had surrounded the whole Valley that seemed like a real possibility. For a while, we heard 33 going north was the only way out of town. And then we heard that was closed.

The next day, someone said 150 to Carpinteria was still open. It seemed like everyone in Ojai headed that way while they still could. They were driving past our house, bumper to bumper. It went on for hours. They constantly had to stop, which meant we could walk alongside the cars and ask why and where they were going. They said they were just getting out. But we didn't want to go.

We bought a couple of air filters, and we even wore our masks inside our house. The black ash kept on building up in the yard, and it flew up into the air every time the wind blew. After the fire passed through Ojai we watched the news day and night as it burned towards Santa Barbara. It broke my heart to see all the trees and vegetation, all the lives and memories that were burning up.

It wasn't until mid-January that we finally returned to Wills Canyon to see what damage the fire had done. It was depressing, especially knowing so well what used to be there. It had been such a nice shady trail under the oak trees, and now there was so much new open space. Many of the familiar trees had burned and fallen. There was ash everywhere, ash that we knew we'd be breathing for months if we tried to run there. We stayed away to protect our lungs.

We finally went back to Wills Canyon on April 29th, four months after the fire. We found an amazing variety of vegetation, so many different kinds of flowers and climbing vines, and shiny poison oak, ferns and grasses. We were delighted to see that a fair amount of the oak canopy high overhead was still intact, especially higher up on the trail. A lot of the leaves were brown from the fire, but even on some trees that were burned black we could see places of healthy new growth. Only time will tell us how many of those trees will survive. The birds are still there, still singing all along the trail, maybe even more birds than before, if that's possible. Now when will the deer and the bears and the coyotes return?

I WANT TO BELIEVE
≈ David Taylor

I have lived in Ojai for two years now, longer than some, but fewer than most. Before I moved here, I had never heard of this town. I had no connection to this land, nor to the various spiritual communities whose adherents are called here. I learned of the so-called energetic vortex after my wife came to visit friends, and her soul was caught up in the beauty, wonder and magic of this community. Of course, I wouldn't have called it that then, all I knew was that she returned from her trip invigorated, enlightened and excited by the prospects of joining a conscious community where a connection to the land, to each other and to a higher purpose was valued, supported and encouraged. Friends proclaimed maxims like *special people are called to Ojai*, *what you plant in Ojai grows* and *Ojai makes you work on your shit*. My wife, who has always had a connection to the ethereal and otherworldly, was in. Me, I was like that

Photograph by Zoe Murdock

old poster in Fox Mulder's office on the X-Files: 'I Want to Believe.'

I want to believe that during the second day of the Thomas Fire, when we'd made the decision to evacuate and caravan with friends out of town, that something larger was happening. As transplants from New York, with no one in Southern California to turn to, I found myself driving up Route 33, my wife, 4-year-old daughter and three dogs crammed into our Jeep. Crates full of photo albums and hard drives, and duffel bags filled with food, clothes and toiletries filled the entire trunk and back seat, rendering the rear view mirror useless. Thankfully I was the caboose in our little caravan of two and was merely responsible for following behind our dear friends as we drove over the Topa Topas. In the mountains there was no cell service, but our destination was well known to them—Santa Clarita—and I was content to have a plan that extended far enough into the future to know we'd be safe from the fires within a few hours' drive. I generally like to be in control of the plan, or at least be a part of the planning process, but in this case I realized there were a lot of emotions in play between my wife and our friends, and I decided to ground myself in doing the job assigned to me: drive my family to safety.

But at the top of the mountains, when our cell service returned, it became clear that this plan wasn't working. In the time it had taken us to drive through the mountains, a new fire had ignited in Santa Clarita. We were now fleeing one fire to head directly into another; I want to believe a larger force was at work, guiding us to San Luis Obispo, where we ultimately landed.

I want to believe that the manager of the Sands Inn and Suites in San Luis Obispo, Matt, was divinely situated to maximize his influence in aiding myself and the hundred or so other Ojai evacuees that found ourselves in his care. When he shared his childhood trauma of losing everything to a fire at the formative age of 13, I knew this man's history guided his actions as he canceled reservations to clear rooms for us, as he brought cots into the conference rooms to provide more people solace, as he reduced room rates dramatically for everyone and their pets and as he gathered supplies from local restaurants, grocers and vineyards and coordinated a community gathering at the hotel pool with everything we would need to begin to relax and take our minds out of the immediate and ongoing fear, trauma and heartache of the devastation wrought by the fires. That night, thanks to this man who I want to believe is an angel, bonds of friendship were born, strangers became neighbors and a community in pain came together.

My wife believes that in those first few days, when the entire town was encompassed in flames, literally a Johnny Cash 'Ring of Fire' surrounding Ojai, that something miraculous occurred, that downtown was protected in a spiritual way.

And I want to believe that too, but I cannot discount the bravery and heroism of the numerous first responders who valiantly and selflessly held the line and fought with their lives to keep as much of our beautiful town safeguarded as they possibly could. Their service is no miracle, it isn't otherworldly, it comes from strength of character, from training, from a sense of service. The parable of the drowning man reminds me that the two are not mutually exclusive. That the thoughts and prayers we were all sending out to the universe were heard, the call to save our town and stop the destruction was taken up by a larger force, was heeded and responded to, from those that could help, from places near and far. And possibly beyond.

I am definitely on a path somewhere, aligning with things that I cannot see but that I can feel. Things that I cannot understand but that I can sense are true. And I want to believe that all of this is connected, that we are all connected. To this land, to each other, to a larger purpose.

Photograph by Zoe Murdock

GRATITUDE AND ACTION
Rabbi Joe Menashe, Camp Ramah

On the morning of Friday, December 8th, as we entered the Ojai Valley, visibility was reduced to a few hundred yards due to the thick pall of smoke from the Thomas Fire, and every breath was shallow and labored. We arrived in Ojai to assess our land and thank the firefighters in person.

What we found was Camp Ramah, smoke-filled and hazy, but perfectly intact with no structural destruction or damage to our buildings. The hills to the north, including hundreds of acres of Ramah's property, were scorched all the way to the fence line. The heroic actions of teams of firefighters on the ground and in the air, along with the providence of a shift in the wind, spared Ramah.

A few years ago, Ojai native, beloved friend of Ramah and Ojai general contractor Scott Lundy and his dad, Ralph (Gramps), placed an owl box over the director's house. Years passed with no visual or audible sign of an owl.

However, a few months following the fire and the devastating change in habitat for the wildlife in the neighboring Los Padres National Forest, a beautiful barn owl has made this perch its home. In Jewish tradition and folklore an owl often finds refuge in ruins or a place of prior devastation. I believe it moved in over my house in part to remind us of these lessons of gratitude and action.

The first lesson the owl teaches is to breathe. One of the biblical names for an owl is *tinshemet*, which in Hebrew is formed by the same root word as breath. Camp Ramah is in Ojai, which is a sacred and unique space that in the frenetic modern world serves as a reminder to recognize blessings and to breathe. Gratitude.

Second, according to the Talmud, an owl, unlike other birds, looks forward like humans. At a time of peril and loss, the owl reminds us to get unstuck. Look toward to the future. Action.

So, this magnificent creature we see in the towering oaks who leaves us near daily remnants of its nighttime activities is a poignant reminder for us all to breathe in a moment of gratitude, and to look to the future in a journey of action.

Gratitude and Action.

Western Screech Owl that has taken up residence in a newly placed owl nesting box, part of the Ojai Raptor Center's Thomas Fire Wildlife Recovery Initiative.

Photograph by Brian Rasnow

PINK CHIEF

The Thomas Fire was a scary time for me. My family and I evacuated on December 5, 2017. We stayed in Paso Robles. The fire had passed above my neighborhood, resulting in mandatory evacuations for my house. The winds were not as strong as they projected and that saved my house from burning down. The ten days that we were evacuated was one of the scariest times I have experienced.

Once we came home, and life settled back down, my dad and I went for a drive during a pink moment. We wanted to see if the pink moment would look different with the burned and bare mountains in Ojai. We stopped and admired Chief Peak during the pink moment behind the green orange groves. It was just as beautiful as before the Thomas Fire with just a different feel, which was very comforting to see. Ojai is still my home despite the damage the Thomas Fire left.

Artwork and writing by Aubrey Larson
Age 10

BORN OF FIRE: THE CRACK AWAKENS THE LIGHT

As Leonard Cohen sang in his song 'Anthem,' *there is a crack, a crack in everything. That's how the light gets in.* Born of fire, millions of years ago, molten lava flowed and burned everything in its path, then cooled forming giant columns of basalt with natural inclusions in the stone. When I was carving this basalt sculpture, an inclusion released its stress and the stone split in two. My original plan was lost by the break so I abandoned these two stone pieces for a number of years. Last summer, while up in Washington at my former carving studio, I was looking at what I had abandoned and I now wanted to complete. I decided to bring this broken sculpture to Ojai and maybe I would have a new idea of what I could make of it. It wasn't until after the fire, while walking through my studio, that I saw the renewed vision. I saw the crack awakening new possibilities. This is how I felt after the Thomas Fire. The fire brought a severe split in the flow of my life and the lives of so many of us. It transformed what was… into the new.

Artwork and writing by Brian Berman

FIRE BOWLS
≥ *Darrel Wilson*

It seems all who live in the Valley use the Thomas Fire as a milepost. Some things were before the fire, others are after. It is a huge experience that we seek to put into its proper place as we move on with our lives. We need perspective and our work is a great step in that direction.

The first night of the fire, my son called from Carpinteria at 1:30 am saying *evacuate right away. What happened in Sonoma County could happen here if the winds go the wrong way.* In 20 minutes we were driving on the 150 to his home. As the road turned east alongside Lake Casitas the entire horizon, side to side, was pure fire. We felt vulnerable, scared and proud that we were escaping its destruction. Of course, we left everything that accumulates with 44 years of marriage, two children and six grandchildren. *It's just stuff, and we are alive,* we reminded ourselves over and over.

Our refuge sheltered seven adults, four young children and five dogs. But the fire pushed on towards Carpinteria, so a couple of days later we relocated to a safer place. With our moves, the two 4-year-olds were deeply worried and repeatedly asked *what will we do if our house burns?* We struggled to explain that if you stay out of harm's way, there is always hope of rebuilding and experiencing the wisdom that comes from passing through loss and grief. And we silently wondered if gaining that perspective would be our journey.

We also thought about the people who were fleeing famine and war in Africa and the Middle East and realized these refugees were experiencing something far worse. These people are brothers and sisters struggling to stay alive, just as we are, but with far more jeopardy and difficulty. That put the question of immigration into a very different, more compassionate context.

When I returned home ten days later, I felt adrift and unsettled. The ash was everywhere and the more I swept up, the more settled in its place. The smoke was constantly irritating; destruction was everywhere. Turning wood is my daily hobby but I couldn't pick it up.

And then a couple of weeks later 21 people perished in the Montecito floods. We thought the fire was terrible, but the loss of life in the floods was far worse. And with new rainstorms, my grandchildren and family had to flee to Ojai several times. What was next?

The flood littered the Carp beach several feet deep with debris and some were charred root burls of ceanothus and manzanita. Their grain is swirly and the finished colors are those of fire which I thought might be perfect for wood turning. They represented the possibility of rebuilding, not as I feared with a home, but rather of finding a way forward through creativity and discovery.

The wood fought me; it was hard to turn and my struggle was intense. I did not have the right tools to transform its charred forms into beauty. Four faceplates (essential lathe tools) broke as I made the bowl for Travis Escalante, each in different ways. I bought new tools and learned new techniques that worked much better. The more I worked, the happier I felt. I was getting my turning mojo back and making beauty. My wife selected a charred chunk and made her own beautiful fire bowl.

In retrospect, this journey is about recovery, gaining new perspectives and defining life after the Thomas Fire milepost.

Bowl by Darrel Wilson

Large bowl by Darrel Wilson
Small bowl by Beth Wilson

Photographs by Laura Whitney
The Ojai Foundation

Two days after we lost our place Shawn said, *we lost our house but we did not lose our home.* I feel—and I speak for our family in saying this—we are blessed to have witnessed and experienced the power of Mother Nature. In the wake of such destruction the beauty of humanity shone through, and in the loss of our former existence we have gathered more humility. We have grown from this experience. We have a deeper understanding of ourselves, others and the integral part we play in being human on Earth.

➤ *Stacey Moss*

What may have seemed lost on the surface of the vegetation that showed blackened limbs and charred bark was, upon closer inspection, found to reveal new bright green tender leaves coming from the base of these very same plants.

➤ *Jack Nesbit*

Photographs by Jack Nesbit

THE TANGIBLE SPIRIT OF THE OJAI VALLEY

The extraordinary qualities of the Ojai Valley are reflected in the land, her people and a tangible spirit of rebirth. All the forces that make her so palpable have been revered, sung and spoken of since time immemorial. A rare geometaphysical work of art wrapped all around the basin, anyone who has been here has felt the enchantment, the breath of Awhay—the moon—and the magnificence of this Valley.

The shapes that make up the area's terrain are key to this unusual energy. A powerhouse of geomagnetic and cosmological Qi, the mountain range encompassing the Valley is an extremely rare landform: mountains shaped and situated in such a way as to generate vital life force energy—*Qi*. These same mountain shapes are recorded in the pages of ancient landform books, poems and songs from venerable Feng Shui tomes—writings that detail otherworldly elevations generating and releasing immense, sublime energies into the local communities. These intense forces are initiated in the Valley by tectonic stress, above and below groundwater, temperature, mineral and quartz content, orientation, shape, physical relation of the mountains to each other, and the extraordinary Qi generated by and exchanged between them.

Fires have torn at the Valley and surrounding wilderness but have yet to destroy them beyond life. They burn violently and scorch black, revealing naked, hunched angular folds and forms, a stunned silence from the land. Yet Springtime 2018 shouted *I live!*, with the return of birds, insects, velvety carpets of chartreuse mountain flowers and baby oak sprouting from pitch and charcoal mother trees. The extraordinary geometaphysical landforms that helped shoulder the Thomas Fire and countless others are now witness and host to the rebirth of the Valley and its extraordinary people.

— Lee Ann Manley
Living Space Feng Shui

Photographs by Elizabeth Rose
December 6, 2017 and March 7, 2018

AN OFFERING

Leave something behind in this ritual of burning.
You will leave everything behind.

Belongings too heavy to carry become remnants,
fragments lived and unlived, and your own belonging remains—
to this earth, this body, this heart, each other.

You will find freedom in touching nothingness,
and find another you in the returning,
moving through the pathless mountains,
knowing lightness and burden,
the giving up,
the longing.

The well of love is the other end of grief,
filling nothingness with stories, and who would we be without them?
Without someone to share them with,
without someone to remind you how nothing lasts,
but it lasts long enough to love.
To keep letting go until nothing is left but the light that started it.

You are the bright breath among blackened branches,
reaching out to your own unseen hands,
the ones that hold the stars, with eyes for the invisible.
And you pull out your heart, again, and let it rest
on a sunlit stone, warm and beating, poised for the next reckoning,
or blessing, or silence. A heart who asks you only to be,
who tells you it will be enough.
You learn how to hold tightly for a time,
because you do not want to turn away from what you know
while it becomes something else.

Love will have you relinquish everything, at some point.
Full bodied emptying before the filling, how fire moves
from roots to trunk and exhales at the top,
how lungs do in a clear-sky dream,
when you take an inhale deep enough to turn green with hope.
You will all push up through the wreckage and grow, and die,
and be something
important in between.

Your resilience is resounding.

Remember,
For you are here for it, for a little bit.
Lucky enough to be. Enough.
You are the little seed who comes to life after the fire.
All together on the hill,
rising through the layered soil of memory,
using it for rising, living, opening.
An offering.

≥ *Emily Burger*

Photograph by Garth Rose

Photograph by Michael Wood

Photograph by Julia Thomsen

Photograph by Emily Vedder

LISTEN

the mountains are revealed
burned black
the outlines
the trails
unobscured
like a face
grown more majestic
by time

from blackest brush
crisp
mournful
do new shoots arise
pushing
vibrating with life
do you hear the sound

someone will wish us
to return to our
old self

but the old self
is dead

and the new self
is so very
very
beautiful

≽ *Susanna Joslyn Johansen*

I became instantly fascinated by the organic misshaping of possessions once dear to us so I began to assemble the discarded results of Thomas's mighty hand. Inspired by the incredible amounts of burnt driftwood that covered the shorelines in the wake of the storms that followed I picked the ones that spoke to me. God had done most of the work and invited me to continue the form resulting in the fiery shapes that graced their demise. For me creating from what is perceived as destruction has been therapeutic in processing such an epic event.

Artwork and writing by Domonic Dean Breaux

WHAT WILL I DO WITH THIS?
≽ Elizabeth Rose

Last week my town burned, as did the towns and cities around me—Santa Paula, Oak View, Casitas Springs, Ventura, Fillmore, Carpinteria, Summerland, Montecito and into Santa Barbara. The fire is named Thomas and it skirted its way over ridges and down into valleys, along highways and roadways and jumped over concrete to reach its hand towards the beach past Mussel Shoals. It rode on Santa Ana winds, fast and focused and moving at speeds that nobody expected. Because this is what fire does. It grew from small to thousands of acres in seven short days. It is burning still as it makes its way along the ridges of national forest land and fills the sky with falling ash.

I think we were some of the first to leave the lower Valley—myself and my husband, my cat and my dog. And our neighbors who live along the road that sits nestled against a hillside and shares its land with Upper Ojai. Vast and open space, Upper Ojai was already burning before we knew there even was a fire. It had come up upon them from opposite where our Valley sits.

When we did know there was a fire, we stayed awake to watch online but finally, at midnight, I could not keep my eyes open and made my way to bed. My dog and I. Only to have my husband wake us up not even an hour later, *Lizzie, we need to evacuate*.

In that moment when I had to think about what was important there was little attachment to anything that was a thing. I had my life partner, my soul dog, my spirit cat. I took our passports because you are always supposed to take your passports. And a folder with our birth certificates because my youngest daughter's name change was in there and the written documentation of her name evolution to Faith was the key to something important. I still am not sure what that is.

My reptilian brain—my primitive, instinctive brain, my powerful and oldest brain—knew what was important, that I only needed those few things. And truthfully, if I had left the bag on the table that would have been okay, too.

We went back home the next day. Tuesday. The fire had not made it down the mountain yet to edge along the land behind my home. We went back home and still only a few things called for me to take them out of harm's way. I grabbed clothing I would need to keep warm when I walked my dog. I took my three pieces of jewelry. And a second pair of jeans to wear if we were gone a long time. And then we were gone. Again.

Tuesday night the fires came. Over the rise from Upper Ojai and down the hillside, mocking the houses that lived against the overgrown branches and grasses that hadn't seen fire for so many years. The fire crews came and saved our home along with a neighbor who stayed on his land, next to ours, and worked alongside our fire angels. I got updates as the night played out against the fire's fitful dance. And I did not know till morning that my house had made it through.

I woke up before morning and walked myself, in my mind's eye, through my house. And saw only a few more things that I should have taken with me. Included in these things were clothes. A pair of pants that I love. And a sweater, too. A dress and a lace shirt that is more like a slip. And just one pair of shoes.

This was no longer that ancient and wise brain thinking now. This was my new and present brain. The brain that puts value on things. The brain that is not just in survival mode but has time to think and process and second-guess, too. And this brain, it still only picked just those few items. Because it knew—because I know—that there are only a very few things, really, in all of the items that we own, that matter that much.

To me they are pieces of clothing. That are more than pieces of clothing. For you they may be a bracelet that was your great aunt's or a painting found in a small shop in a sweet town in a country far from ours. Maybe it is that handprint of your child when they were young or a photograph at your wedding or the newspaper eulogy of your mom or dad.

What we value is so deep in us. And so unique to us. And the gift that is this burning is that it rids us—just as it clears away the

Photograph by Ellyn Jarvis

underbrush so that we can see the dirt below—of the superficial. This burning is a cleansing. And now we see what is important.

But what will I do with this? In what direction will I walk, as I walk the scarred and ash-filled land above my home? What will move me forward as I help move forward those who lost so much more than me? Where will I put

my focus, my intention, my passion and my energy as I focus love and support on this town that sat within a circle of fire? How will I best make use of all that I have learned from all that we have (lost) found. Because from this burning comes opportunity. And possibility. And new growth. Always new growth.

FIRST SUNSET HIKE

I had a bit of fear in my heart to go up and see the scorched hills, but I can say that it was the most exhilarating, exciting, beautiful hiking experience I've had here in years. The hills, naked and ravaged and scarred, laid bare in front of me in muted color harmony. The lovely golds and reds and greys that are always there, but now accentuated with black and white, like a finely outlined painting. I could see each rock, each curve of the mountains, each trampled pathway, normally hidden from view by the foliage that has now been burnt away. It was exciting to walk the path of the fire and see how it jumps, how it follows the water lines, how it transforms the landscape in glorious ways. The fear in my heart quickly turned to joy and everything felt *right* somehow. Blackened. Greyed out. Yet so colorful and majestic. So raw. So blank. So ready for new life. I even came across some pyrophytic plants and a family of deer. To see the life in the destruction, the beauty in chaos, the newness springing forth from the death of the old.

Photograph and writing by Pamela Luna

Paul Bergmann
Ojai Valley Community Church
July 14, 2018

I went to bed concerned for my friends in Santa Paula and believing that the fire would be handled. But on Tuesday, at about 8:00 am, Kathy tries to wake me up, *you know that fire... we should think about leaving.*

    This was a day off from work for me and our kids were home and when we sleep in, we sleep in. And Kathy tries to wake me again at 9:00, *honey, I...* And, I am, like, *Kath, the phone alerts would be going off, someone would be calling us.* And she says, *I think you should take a look* and I'm like, *it's fine, it's fine.* Then at 10:00, she wakes me with, *get out of the f#@%ing bed.*

    I jump up asking what is going on and she says, *just go outside and look,* and so I go onto my front porch and look toward Soule Park Golf Course and I see an absolute wall of smoke going 1000 feet in the air. I could not believe what I was seeing. And then I'm hysterical, *we've got to get out of here!*

    I'm waking up the kids and yelling at my wife to start getting things together and we're getting information and calling people and realizing the scope of this fire. I call my daughter in Santa Barbara and she says not to come there. That it's a mess already. I call some friends who are driving out and learn that the 33 is backed up and the 150 is backed up. We aren't sure where to go.

    We begin the process of deciding what to bring with us. It comes down to those things that have meaning to us. Not just the jewelry for money's sake but my mom's ring and Kathy's mom's ring and my kid's instruments. They took their favorite because they could not take every one. I looked at boxes of clippings and articles from my football career and realized, *I don't need this.* That was really cathartic to learn what was important during this experience.

    We decide to take the 33 to Bakersfield. We connect with some good friends. It is us and them and all our kids and our four dogs. The hotel we found had other Ojai folks. I met a family a few doors down from us and it turned out they lived three doors down from us here in Ojai. It took this fire to meet each other.

    We came back to Ojai three days later. I have my church that I needed to get back to. To drive into Ojai, we had to circle around and take the 101 to the 33 up through Casitas Springs. There was so much devastation and then we started to see all the homes that were saved. It was incredible to see the scope of the fire and see the amount of structures that survived.

    The first Sunday after the fire, our building was full of ash and smoke and there was no way to meet there. That second weekend, I'm looking over at Soule Park and thinking that they have got to be hurting, that their business is nonexistent right now and I had the idea to hold church there, at the restaurant there. I called the manger and said, *hey, I'm thinking about this Sunday, that I'd like to bring my church over to the bar and grill. It's not going to be a big religious message, it's a gathering and I'll buy everyone food and drinks—mimosas and Bloody Marys—and I am betting that you are hurting, and so what do you think?* And there is silence on the other end. And I think he doesn't like the idea much and then I realize he is really emotional and he says that this is the most unbelievable thing and that was it. We had church there and it was amazing.

    We were surrounded by that green lawn, which felt really good. And the waiters and bartenders and staff were just great. And everyone showed up. And tipped extra well. It was a good feeling all around. And this was the moment for me when I knew that we would rebound. Not just my people in church but our community on that macro level. We needed to be together. We needed to be with our people. To feel that connection.

    This book does that. It connects the community together so many months after the fire. And hopefully for a long time after that. There is this deep and intrinsic value of remembering and this book allows you to do that. Because in our multimedia lives we can move on really fast, but this experience that we all had, it's still right there, under the surface. It's being masked. There is PTSD and trauma. We need to stop and reflect and remember.

    When the air quality finally got good, a couple of months later, Kathy and I went for a hike for the first time in a while to our hiking trails that we do off of Shelf Road. There was some green that was sprouting back, wrapping around the charred branches, and the Earth was bouncing back. That, for me, is spirituality. Seeing the growth just spoke so deep to my heart because this is what I believe, I believe in the end, love wins. I believe that somehow, despite all the negativity and the bad things happening in the world, the best thing that has ever been under the sun is love and it's going to win in the end. It's going to have the last word. Not brokenness and corruption and pain and evil but love. Love is going to win.

    I believe that for each and every one of us, whatever happens at the end when we die, we're going to transition into that love. I don't know what that looks like, some people say it's heaven, some people say it's being reabsorbed into the wonder of the cosmos. Whatever it is, I believe it is good and I believe it's going to be the winner. So, when I saw the green coming back out of the ashes, that cycle of life-death-rebirth, life-death-rebirth that plays out in seasons, it was playing out right here. It is a metaphor for life. Life wins. Life wins. It comes back. It comes back. It is very powerful for me. Wherever you are in your life, something green is going to come and wrap you up and grow in love.

Photograph by Nathan Wickstrum
Ventura River Preserve

ELIZABETH ROSE

Elizabeth immediately noticed the beautiful poetry and prose that arose from the Thomas Fire and envisioned a book coming out of the fire to honor the experiences that the Ojai Valley shared. She created a Facebook page—WritingFromTheFire—and invited the community to come together with their words. Shortly after, Elizabeth found Deva's post about her desire to create a photography book and she reached out, *either you read my mind or I read yours!* This collaboration with Deva and the making of FROM THE FIRE is preceded by an eclectic background. Elizabeth is an attorney with a mediation practice helping couples to end their marriage while sustaining their family. She is an editor and works with other writers to ensure that their words are clear and strong. And she writes a popular blog—IveJustGottaSayThis.com—that captures the life of a midlife woman. Elizabeth is a Mother, Partner, Friend, Sister, Daughter, Dancer, Dog and Cat Lover. She grew up in New York, raised her three children in Massachusetts and she currently lives in Ojai with her husband, her soul dog and her spirit cat.

DEVA TEMPLE

Deva felt compelled to create a photography book to capture the deep experiences shared by her community. She was moved by the outpouring of love and support she witnessed in Ojai as the fire burned and in the days after. She wanted to create a book that would challenge the story of human selfishness that we absorb from our culture. She believes that all humans have a need for connection and that altruism is inherent in who we are. Along with her work on this book, Deva teaches yoga-informed, body-focused trauma transformation and leads grief integration rites of passage as well as offering lifestyle courses on authenticity, self love and self actualization. Her writing can be found online at BlissfulWomanhood.com and at HerHeartSpeaks.com. Her work straddles and integrates three worlds: the personal, the collective and the transcendent. Deva holds a BA in Psychology from Lewis & Clark College and an MA in Global Leadership and Sustainable Development from Hawaii Pacific University. She grew up in Ojai and currently lives with her husband, four dogs and many chickens in Ashland, Oregon.

Photograph by Deva Temple
Thomas Aquinas College